RECONSTRUCTION IN PHILOSOPHY

RECONSTRUCTION IN PHILOSOPHY

By

JOHN DEWEY

Enlarged Edition

WITH A NEW INTRODUCTION
BY THE AUTHOR

THE BEACON PRESS · BOSTON

INTRODUCTION

RECONSTRUCTION AS SEEN TWENTY–FIVE YEARS LATER

I

THE TEXT of this volume was written some twenty-five years ago—that is, soon after the First World War; that text is printed without revision. This Introduction is written in the spirit of the text. It is also written in the firm belief that the events of the intervening years have created a situation in which the need for reconstruction is vastly more urgent than when the book was composed; and, more specifically, in the conviction that the present situation indicates with greatly increased clearness where the needed reconstruction must center, the locus from which detailed new developments must proceed. Today Reconstruction *of* Philosophy is a more suitable title than Reconstruction *in* Philosophy. For the intervening events have sharply defined, have brought to a head, the basic postulate of the text: namely, that the distinctive office, problems and subjectmatter of philosophy grow out of stresses and strains in the community life in which a given form of philosophy arises, and that, accordingly, its specific problems vary with the changes in human life that are always going on and that at times constitute a crisis and a turning point in human history.

The First World War was a decided shock to the earlier period of optimism, in which there prevailed widespread belief in continued progress toward mutual understanding among peoples and classes, and hence a sure movement to harmony and peace. Today the shock is almost incredibly greater. Insecurity and strife are so general that the prevailing attitude is one of anxious and pessimistic uncertainty. Uncertainty as to what the future has in store casts its heavy and black shadow over all aspects of the present.

In philosophy today there are not many who exhibit confidence about its ability to deal competently with the serious issues of the day. Lack of confidence is manifested in concern for the improvement of techniques, and in threshing over the systems of the past. Both of these interests are justifiable in a way. But with respect to the first, the way of reconstruction is not through giving attention to form at the expense of substantial content, as is the case with techniques that are used only to develop and refine still more purely formal skills. With respect to the second, the way is not through increase of erudite scholarship about the past that throws no light upon the issues now troubling mankind. It is not too much to say that, as far as interest in the two topics just mentioned predominates, the withdrawal from the present scene, increasingly evident in philosophy, is itself a sign of the extent of the disturbance and unsettlement that now marks the other aspects of man's life. Indeed, we may go farther and say that such withdrawal is one manifestation of just those defects of past systems that render them of little value for the troubled affairs of the present: namely, the desire to find something so fixed and certain as to provide a secure refuge. The problems with which a philosophy relevant to the present must deal are those growing out of changes going on with ever-increasing rapidity, over an ever-increasing human-geographical range, and with ever-deepening intensity of penetration; this fact is one striking indication of the need for a very different kind of reconstruction from that which is now most in evidence.

When a view similar to that here presented has been advanced on previous occasions, as, indeed, in the text which follows, it has been criticized as taking what one of the milder of my critics has called "a sour attitude" toward the great systems of the past. It is, accordingly, relevant to the theme of needed reconstruction to say that the adverse criticisms of philosophies of the past are not directed at these systems with respect to their connection with intellectual and moral issues of their own time and place, but with respect to their relevancy in a much changed human situation. The very things

that made the great systems objects of esteem and admiration in their own socio-cultural contexts are in
large measure the very grounds that deprive them of
"actuality" in a world whose main features are different
to an extent indicated by our speaking of the "scientific revolution," the "industrial revolution" and the
"political revolution" of the last few hundred years. A
plea for reconstruction cannot, as far as I can see, be
made without giving considerable critical attention to
the background within which and in regard to which
reconstruction is to take place. Far from being a sign
of disesteem, this critical attention is an indispensable
part of interest in the development of a philosophy
that will do for our time and place what the great doctrines of the past did in and for the cultural media out
of which they arose.

Another criticism akin to that just discussed is that
the view here taken of the work and office of philosophy
rests upon a romantic exaggeration of what can be accomplished by "intelligence." If the latter word were
used as a synonym for what one important school of
past ages called "reason" or "pure intellect," the
criticism would be more than justified. But the word
names something very different from what is regarded
as the highest organ or "faculty" for laying hold of ultimate truths. It is a shorthand designation for great
and ever-growing methods of observation, experiment

and reflective reasoning which have in a very short time revolutionized the physical and, to a considerable degree, the physiological conditions of life, but which have not as yet been worked out for application to what is itself distinctively and basically *human*. It is a newcomer even in the physical field of inquiry; as yet it hasn't developed in the various aspects of the human scene. The reconstruction to be undertaken is not that of applying "intelligence" as something readymade. It is to carry over into any inquiry into human and moral subjects the kind of method (the method of observation, theory as hypothesis, and experimental test) by which understanding of physical nature has been brought to its present pitch.

Just as theories of knowing that developed prior to the existence of scientific inquiry provide no pattern or model for a theory of knowing based upon the present actual conduct of inquiry, so the earlier systems reflect both pre-scientific views of the natural world and also the pre-technological state of industry and the pre-democratic state of politics of the period when their doctrines took form. The actual conditions of life in Greece, particularly in Athens, when classic European philosophy was formulated set up a sharp division between doing and knowing, which was generalized into a complete separation of theory and "practice." It reflected, at the time, the economic organization in which "useful" work was done for the most part by slaves, leaving free men relieved from labor and "free" on that account. That such a state of affairs is also pre-democratic is clear. In political matters, nevertheless, philosophers retained the separation of theory and practice long after tools and processes derived from industrial operations had become indispensable resources in conducting the observations and experiments that are the heart of scientific knowing.

It should be reasonably obvious that an important aspect of the reconstruction that now needs to be carried out concerns the theory of knowledge. In it a radical change is demanded as to the subjectmatter upon which that theory must be based; the new theory will consider how knowing (that is, inquiry that is competent) is carried on, instead of supposing that it must be made to conform to views independently formed regarding faculties of organs. And, while substitution of "intelligence," in the sense just indicated, for "reason" is an important element in the change demanded, reconstruction is not confined to that matter. For the so-called "empirical" theories of knowledge, though they rejected the position of the rationalist school, operated in terms of what *they* took to be a necessary and sufficient faculty of knowledge, accommodating the theory of knowing to their preformed beliefs about "sense-perception" instead of deriving their view of sense-perception from what goes on in the conduct of scientific inquiry.[1]

It will be noted that the adverse criticisms dealt with in the foregoing paragraphs are dealt with not for the sake of replying to criticisms, but primarily as illustrations of why reconstruction is urgently required, and secondarily as illustrations of where it is needed. For there is no promise of the rise and growth of a philosophy relevant to the conditions that *now* supply the materials of philosophical issues and problems, save as the work of reconstruction takes serious account of how and where systems of the past indicate the need for reconstruction in the present.

II

It has been stated that philosophy grows out of, and in intention is connected with, human affairs. There is implicit in this view the further view that, while acknowledgment of this fact is a precondition of the reconstruction now required, yet it means more than that philosophy *ought* in the future to be connected with the crises and tensions in the conduct of human affairs. For

---

[1] The obvious insufficiency of psychological theories on this point has played a part in developing the formalisms already noted. Instead of using this insufficiency as ground for reconstruction of the psychological theory, the defective view was accepted qua psychology and hence was used as a ground for a "logical" theory of knowing that shut out entirely all reference to the factual ways in which knowledge advances.

it is held that in effect, if not in profession, the great systems of Western philosophy all have been thus motivated and occupied. A claim that they always have been sufficiently aware of what they were engaged in would, of course, be absurd. They have seen themselves, and have represented themselves to the public, as dealing with something which has variously been termed Being, Nature or the Universe, the Cosmos at large, Reality, the Truth. Whatever names were used, they had one thing in common: they were used to designate something taken to be fixed, immutable, and therefore out of time; that is, eternal. In being also something conceived to be universal or all-inclusive, this eternal being was taken to be above and beyond all variations in space. In this matter, philosophers reflected in generalized form the popular beliefs which were current when events were thought of as taking place *in* space and time as their all-comprehensive envelopes. It is a familiar fact that the men who initiated the revolution in natural science held that space and time were independent of each other and of the things that exist and the events that take place within them. Since the assumption of underlying fixities—of which the matter of space and time and of immutable atoms is an exemplification—dominated "natural" science, there is no ground for surprise that in a more generalized form it was the foundation upon which philosophy assumed, as a matter of course, that it must erect its structure. Philosophical doctrines which disagreed about virtually everything else were at one in the assumption that their distinctive concern as philosophy was to search for the immutable and ultimate—that which *is*—without respect to the temporal or spatial. Into this state of affairs in natural science as well as in moral standards and principles, there recently entered the discovery that natural science is forced by its own development to abandon the assumption of fixity and to recognize that what for it is actually "universal" is *process;* but this fact of recent science still remains in philosophy, as in popular opinion up to the present time, a technical matter rather than what it is: namely, the most revolutionary discovery yet made.

The supposed fact that morals demand immutable, extra-temporal principles, standards, norms, ends, as the only assured protection against moral chaos can, however, no longer appeal to natural science for its support, nor expect to justify by science its exemption of morals (in practice and in theory) from considerations of time and place—that is, from processes of change. Emotional—or sentimental—reaction will doubtless continue to resist acknowledgment of this fact and refuse to use in morals the standpoint and outlook which have now made their way into natural science. But in any case, science and traditional morals have been at complete odds with one another as to the kinds of things which, according to one and the other, are immutable. Hence a deep and impassable gulf is set up between the *natural* subjectmatter of science and the *extra-* if not *supra-*natural subjectmatter of morals. There must be many thoughtful persons who are so dismayed by the inevitable consequences of this split that they will welcome that change in point of view which will render the methods and conclusions of natural science serviceable for moral theory and practice. All that is needed is acceptance of the view that moral subjectmatter is also spatially and temporally qualified. Considering the controverted present state of morals and its loss of popular esteem, the sacrifice demanded should not seem threatening to those who are not moved by vested institutional interest. As for philosophy, its profession of operating on the basis of the eternal and the immutable is what commits it to a function and a subjectmatter which, more than anything else, are the source of the growing popular disesteem and distrust of its pretensions; for it operates under cover of what is now repudiated in science, and with effective support only from old institutions whose prestige, influence and emoluments of power depend upon the preservation of the old order; and this at the very time when human conditions are so disturbed and unsettled as to call more urgently than at any previous time for the kind of comprehensive and "objective" survey in which historic philosophies have engaged. To the vested interests, maintenance of belief in the transcendence of space and time, and hence the derogation of what is "merely" human, is an indispensable prerequisite of their retention of an authority which in practice is translated into power to regulate human affairs throughout—from top to bottom.

There is, however, such a thing as relative—that is *relational*—universality. The actual conditions and occasions of human life differ widely with respect to their comprehensiveness in range and in depth of penetration. To see why such is the case, one does not have to depend upon a scientifically exploded theory of control from outside and above by self-moved and self-moving forces. On the contrary, theory began to count in the sciences of astronomy, physics, physiology, in their multiple and varied aspects, when this attitude of dogmatism was replaced by the use of hypotheses in conducting experimental observations to bind concrete facts together in systems of increasing temporal-spatial extent. The *universality* that belongs to scientific theories is not that of inherent content fixed by God or Nature, but of range of applicability—of capacity to take events out of their apparent isolation so as to order them into systems which (as is the case with all living things) prove they are alive by the kind of change which is *growth*. From the standpoint of scientific inquiry nothing is more fatal to its right to obtain acceptance than a claim that its conclusions are final and hence incapable of a development that is other than mere quantitative extension.

While I was engaged in writing this Introduction, I received a copy of an address recently delivered by a distinguished English man of science. Speaking specifically of science, he remarked, "Scientific discovery is often carelessly looked upon as the creation of some new knowledge which can be added to the great body of old knowledge. This is true of the strictly trivial discoveries. It is not true of the fundamental discoveries, such as those of the laws of mechanics, of chemical combination, of evolution, on which scientific advance ultimately depends. These always entail the destruction of or disintegration of old knowledge *before the new can be created*." [2] He continued by pointing out specific instances of the importance of getting outside of the grooves into which the heavy arm of custom tends to push every form of human activity, not excluding intellectual and scientific inquiry: "It is no accident that bacteria were first understood by a canal engineer, that oxygen was isolated by a Unitarian minister, that the

---

[2] C. D. Darlington, Conway Memorial Lecture on *The Conflict of Society and Science* (London: Watts & Co., 1948); italics not in text.

theory of infection was established by a chemist, the
theory of heredity by a monastic school teacher, and
the theory of evolution by a man who was unfitted to
be a university instructor in either botany or zoology."
He closed by saying, "We need a Ministry of Disturbance, a regulated source of annoyance; a destroyer of
routine; an underminer of complacency." The routine
of custom tends to deaden even scientific inquiry; it
stands in the way of *discovery* and of the *active* scientific worker. For discovery and inquiry are synonymous as an occupation. Science is a *pursuit*, not a
coming into possession of the immutable; new theories
as points of view are more prized than discoveries
that quantitatively increase the store on hand. It is
relevant to the theme of domination by custom that the
lecturer said the great innovators in science "are the
first to fear and doubt their discoveries."

I am here specially concerned with the bearing of
what was said about men of science upon the work of
philosophy. The borderline between what is called hypothesis in science and what is called speculation (usually in a tone of disparagement) in philosophy is thin
and shadowy at the time of initiation of new movements
—those placed in contrast with "technical applications
and developments" such as take place as a matter of
course after a new and revolutionary outlook has managed to win acceptance. Viewed in their own cultural

contexts, the "hypotheses" advanced by those who now
bear the name of great philosophers differ from the
"speculations" of the men who have made great (and
"destructive") innovations in science by having a wider
range of reference and possible application; by the
fact that they claim not to be "technical" but deeply
and broadly human. At the time there is no sure way
of telling whether the new way of seeing and of treating
things is to turn out to be a case of science or of philosophy. Later, the classification is usually made with
comparative ease. It is a case of "science" if and when
its field of application is so specific, so limited, that passage into it is comparatively direct—in spite of the emotional uproar attending its appearance—as, for example, in the case of Darwin's theory. It is designated
"philosophy" when its area of application is so comprehensive that it is not possible for it to pass directly
into formulations of such form and content as to be
serviceable in immediate conduct of specific inquiry.
This fact does not signify its futility; on the contrary,
the contemporary state of cultural conditions was
such as to stand effectually in the way of the development of hypotheses that would give immediate direction to specific observations and experiments so definitely factual as to constitute "science." As the history of scientific inquiry clearly shows, it was during
the "modern" period that inquiry took the form of *dis-*

cussion, which, however, was not useless or idle, scientifically speaking. For, as the word etymologically implies, this discussion was a shaking up, a stirring, which loosened the firm hold of earlier cosmology upon science. This period of discussion, with the loosening that attended it, marks the time of the shading off of what now ranks as "philosophy" into what has now attained the rank of "science." [3] What is called the "climate of opinion" is more than a matter of opinions; it is a matter of cultural habits that determine intellectual as well as emotional and volitional attitudes. The work done by the men whose names now appear in histories of philosophy rather than of science played a large role in producing a climate that was favorable to initiation of the scientific movement whose outcome is the astronomy and physics that have displaced the old ontological cosmology.

It does not need deep scholarship to be aware that, at the time, this new science was regarded as a deliberate assault upon religion and upon the morals then intimately tied up with the religion of Western Europe. Similar attacks followed the revolution that began in the nineteenth century in biology. Historical facts prove

---

[3] It is well worth while recalling that for quite a while Newton ranked as "philosopher" of the division of that subject still classified as "natural" in distinction from metaphysical and moral. Even by his followers his deviations from Descartes were treated as matter not of physical science but of "natural philosophy."

that discussions that have not been carried, because
of their very comprehensive and penetrating scope, to
the point of detail characteristic of science, have done a
work without which science would not be what it now is.

III

The point of the foregoing discussion does not lie,
however, in its bearing upon the value of past philosophic doctrines. Its relevancy for this Introduction
consists of its bearing upon the reconstruction of work
and subjectmatter that is needed to give philosophy
today the vitality once possessed by its predecessors.
What took place in the earlier history of science was
serious enough to be named the "warfare of science and
religion." Nevertheless, the scope of the events that bear
that name is limited, almost technical, when it is placed
in comparison with what is going on now because of
the entry of science more generally into life. The present reach and thrust of what originates as science affects disturbingly every aspect of contemporary life,
from the state of the family and the position of women
and children, through the conduct and problems of education, through the fine as well as the industrial arts,
into political and economic relations of association that
are national and international in scope. They are so
varied, so multiple, as well as developing with such rapidity, that they do not lend themselves to generalized

statement. Moreover, their occurrence presents so many and such serious practical issues demanding immediate attention that man has been kept too busy meeting them piecemeal to make a generalized or intellectual observation of them. They came upon us like a thief in the night, taking us unawares.

The primary requisite of reconstruction is accordingly to arrive at an hypothesis as to how this great change came about so widely, so deeply, and so rapidly. The hypothesis here offered is that the upsets which, taken together, constitute the crisis in which man is now involved all over the world, in all aspects of his life, are due to the entrance into the conduct of the everyday affairs of life of processes, materials and interests whose origin lies in the work done by physical inquirers in the relatively aloof and remote technical workshops known as laboratories. It is no longer a matter of disturbance of religious beliefs and practices, but of every institution established before the rise of modern science a few short centuries ago. The earlier "warfare" was ended not by an out-and-out victory of either of the contestants but by a compromise taking the form of a division of fields and jurisdictions. In moral and ideal matters supremacy was accorded to the old. They remained virtually immutable in their older form. As the uses of the new science proved beneficial in many practical affairs, the new physical and physiological science was tolerated with the understanding that it dealt only with lower material concerns and refrained from entering the higher spiritual "realm" of Being. This "settlement" by the device of division gave rise to the dualisms which have been the chief concern of "modern" philosophy. In the developments which have actually occurred and which have culminated especially within the last generation, the settlement by division of territories and jurisdictions has completely broken down in practice. This fact is exhibited in the present vigorous and aggressive campaign of those who accept the division between the "material" and the "spiritual" but who also hold that the representatives of natural science have not stayed where they belong but have usurped in actual practice—and oftentimes in theory—the right to determine the attitudes and procedures proper to the "higher" authority. Hence, according to them, the present scene of disorder, insecurity and uncertainty, with the strife and anxiety that inevitably results.

I am not here concerned to argue directly against this view. Indeed, it may even be welcomed provided it is taken as an indication of where the issue centers with respect to reconstruction in philosophy. For it indicates by contrast the only direction which, under existing conditions, is intellectually and morally open. The net conclusion of those who hold natural science to be the *fons et origo* of the undeniably serious ills of the present is the necessity of bringing science under subjection to some special institutional "authority." The alternative is a generalized reconstruction so fundamental that it has to be developed by recognition that while the evils resulting at present from the entrance of "science" into our common ways of living are undeniable they are due to the fact that no systematic efforts have as yet been made to subject the "morals" underlying old institutional customs to scientific inquiry and criticism. Here, then, lies the reconstructive work to be done by philosophy. It must undertake to do for the development of inquiry into human affairs and hence into morals what the philosophers of the last few centuries did for promotion of scientific inquiry in physical and physiological conditions and aspects of human life.

This view of what philosophy needs in order to be relevant to present human affairs and to regain the vitality it is losing is not concerned to deny that the entry of science into human activities and interests has its destructive phase. Indeed, the point of departure for the view here presented regarding the reconstruction demanded in philosophy is that this entry, amounting to a hostile invasion of the old, is the main factor operating to produce the present estate of man. And, while the attack upon science as the responsible and guilty party is terribly one-sided in its emphasis upon the destruction involved and in neglect of the many and great human benefits that have accrued, it is held that the issue cannot be disposed of by drawing a balance sheet of human loss and gain with a view to showing that the latter predominates.

The case in fact is much simpler. The premise on which the present assault upon science depends is that old institutional customs, including institutional belief, provide an adequate, and indeed a final, criterion by which to judge the worth of consequences produced by the disturbing entry of science. Those who maintain this premise systematically refuse to note that "science" has a copartner in producing our critical situation. It only takes an eye single to the facts to observe that science, instead of operating alone and in a void, works within an institutional state of affairs developed in pre-scientific days, one which is not modified by scientific inquiry into the moral principles that were then formed and were, presumably, appropriate to it.

One simple example shows the defection and distortion that results from viewing science in isolation. The destructive use made of the fission of the nucleus of an atom has become the stock-in-trade of the assault upon science. What is so ignored as to be denied is that this destructive consequence occurred not only in a war but because of the existence of war, and that war as an institution antedates by unknown millennia the appearance

on the human scene of anything remotely resembling
scientific inquiry. That *in this case* destructive consequences are directly due to pre-existent institutional
conditions is too obvious to call for argument. It does
not prove that such is the case everywhere and at all
times; but it certainly cautions us against the irresponsible and indiscriminate dogmatism now current.
It gives us the definite advice to recall the unscientific
conditions under which morals, in both the practical and
the theoretical senses of that word, took on form and
content. The end-in-view in calling attention to a fact
that cannot be denied, but that is systematically ignored, is not the futile, because totally irrelevant,
purpose of justifying the work of scientific inquirers
in general or in special cases. It is to direct attention
to a fact of outstanding intellectual import. The development of scientific inquiry is immature; it has not
as yet got beyond the physical and physiological aspects
of human concerns, interests and subjectmatters. In
consequence, it has partial and exaggerated effects.
*The institutional conditions into which it enters and
which determine its human consequences have not as yet
been subjected to any serious, systematic inquiry worthy
of being designated scientific.*

The bearing of this state of affairs upon the present
state of philosophy and the reconstruction which should
be undertaken is the theme and thesis of this Introduc-

tion. Before directly resuming that theme, I shall say
something about the present state of morals: a word,
be it remembered, that stands both for a morality as a
practical socio-cultural *fact* in respect to matters of
right and wrong, good and evil, and for theories about
the ends, standards, principles according to which the
actual state of affairs is to be surveyed and judged.
Now the simple fact of the case is that any inquiry into
what is deeply and inclusively human enters perforce
into the specific area of morals. It does so whether it
intends to and whether it is even aware of it or not.
When "sociological" theory withdraws from consideration of the basic interests, concerns, the actively moving aims, of a human culture on the ground that "values" are involved and that inquiry as "scientific" has
nothing to do with values, the inevitable consequence
is that inquiry in the human area is confined to what is
superficial and comparatively trivial, no matter what
its parade of technical skills. But, on the other hand,
if and when inquiry attempts to enter in critical fashion into that which is human in its full sense, it comes
up against the body of prejudices, traditions and institutional customs that consolidated and hardened in a
pre-scientific age. For it is tautology, not the announce-
ment of a discovery or of an inference, to state that
morals, in both senses of the word, are pre-scientific
when formed in an age preceding the rise of science as

now understood and practiced. And to be unscientific, when human affairs in the concrete are immensely altered, is in effect to resist the formation of methods of inquiry into morals in a way that renders existing morals—again in both senses—anti-scientific.

The case would be comparatively simple if there were already in hand the intellectual standpoint, outlook, or what philosophy has called "categories," to serve as instrumentalities of inquiry. But to assume that they are at hand is to assume that intellectual growths which reflect a pre-scientific state of human affairs, concerns, interests and ends are adequate to deal with a human situation which is increasingly and for a very large part the outgrowth of new science. In a word, it is to decide to continue the present state of drift, instability and uncertainty. If the foregoing statements are understood in the sense in which they are intended, the view that is here proposed in regard to reconstruction in philosophy will stand out forcibly. From the position here taken, reconstruction can be nothing less than the work of developing, of forming, of producing (in the literal sense of that word) the intellectual instrumentalities which will progressively direct inquiry into the deeply and inclusively human—that is to say, moral—facts of the present scene and situation.

The first step, a prerequisite of further steps in the same general direction, will be to recognize that, factu-

ally speaking, the present human scene, for good and
evil, for harm and benefit alike, is what it is because,
as has been said, of the entry into everyday and common
(in the sense of ordinary and of shared) ways of living
of what has its origin in *physical* inquiry. The methods and conclusions of "science" do not remain penned
in within "science." Even those who conceive of science
as if it were a self-enclosed, self-actuated independent
and isolated entity cannot deny that it does not remain
such in practical fact. It is a piece of theoretical ani-
mistic mythology to view it as an entity, as do those
who hold that it is *fons et origo* of present human
woes. The science that has so far found its way deeply
and widely into the actual affairs of human life is partial and incomplete science: competent in respect to
physical, and now increasingly to physiological, conditions (as is seen in the recent developments in medicine and public sanitation), but nonexistent with respect
to matters of supreme significance to man—those which
are distinctively of, for, and by, man. No intelligent
way of seeing and understanding the present estate of
man will fail to note the extraordinary split in life occasioned by the radical incompatibility between operations that manifest and perpetuate the morals of a pre-
scientific age and the operations of a scene which has
suddenly, with immense acceleration and with thorough
pervasiveness, been factually determined by a science

which is still partial, incomplete, and of necessity one-sided in operation.

IV

In what precedes, reference has been made several times to what certain human beings classed as philosophers accomplished in the seventeenth, eighteenth and nineteenth centuries in the way of clearing the ground of cosmological and ontological debris which had been absorbed emotionally and intellectually into the very structure and operation of Western culture. It was not claimed that credit for the specific inquiries which progressively revolutionized astronomy, physics (including chemistry) and physiology belongs to philosophers. It is recorded as matter of historic fact that the latter performed an office that, given the accepted cultural climate and the momentum of accepted custom, was an indispensable prerequisite of what men of science accomplished. What will now be added to that statement, in conjunction with its bearing upon reconstruction of philosophy, is that in doing their specific jobs scientific men worked out a method of inquiry so inclusive in range and so penetrating, so pervasive and so universal, as to provide the pattern and model which permits, invites and even demands the kind of formulation that falls within the function of philosophy. It is a method of knowing that is self-corrective in operation;

that learns from failures as from successes. The heart
of the method is the discovery of the identity of inquiry
with discovery. Within the specialized, the relatively
technical, activities of natural science, this office of discovery, of uncovering the new and leaving behind the
old, is taken for granted. Its similar centrality in every
form of intellectual activity is, however, so far from
enjoying general recognition that, in matters which
are set apart as "spiritual" and "ideal" and as distinctively moral, the mere idea of it shocks many who
take it as a matter of course in their own specialized
work. It is a familiar fact that the practical correlate
of discovery when it is scientific and theoretical is *invention,* and that in many of the physical aspects of
human affairs there is even now a generalized method
for the invention of inventions. In what is distinctively
human, invention rarely occurs, and then only in the
stress of an emergency. In human affairs and in
relations that range extensively and penetrate deeply
the mere idea of invention awakens fear and horror,
being regarded as dangerous and destructive. This
fact, which is important but which rarely receives notice, is assumed to belong to the very nature and essence
of morals as morals. This fact testifies both to the reconstruction to be undertaken and to the extreme difficulty of every attempt to bring it about.

The adjustment which finally moderated, without

completely exorcising, the earlier split between science and received institutional customs was a truce rather than anything remotely approaching integration. It consisted, in fact, of a device that was the exact opposite of integration. It operated on the basis of a hard and fast division of the interests, concerns and purposes of human activity into two "realms," or, by a curious use of language, into two "spheres"—not hemispheres. One was taken to be "high" and hence to possess supreme jurisdiction over the other as inherently "low." That which is high was given the name "spiritual," ideal, and was identified with the moral. The other was the "physical" as determined by the procedures of the new science of nature. In being low it was material; its methods were fitted only to the materialistic and to the world of sense-perception, not to that of reason and revelation. The new natural science was grudgingly given a license to operate on condition that it stay in its own compartment and mind its own business, as thus determined for it. That for philosophy the outcome was the whole brood and nest of dualisms which have, upon the whole, formed the "problems" of philosophy termed "modern" is a reflection of the cultural conditions which account for the basic split made between the moral and the physical. These words stand in fact for the attempt to obtain the practical advantages of ease, comfort, convenience and power that were the

outcome of the "application" of the new science to
the ordinary affairs of life, while retaining intact the
supreme authority of the old in those matters of high
morals named "spiritual." The material and utilitarian advantages of the new science, rather than anything approaching acknowledgment of the intellectual
—to say nothing of the moral—import of the new
method, turned out to be the most dependable ally of
the men who produced the new method of revolution-
izing what had been taken to be a scientific account of
nature as cosmos.

The truce endured for a time. The equilibrium it
presented was decidedly uneasy. The saying about
keeping a cake and at the same time eating it is applicable. It represented the effort to enjoy the material
and practical or utilitarian advantages of the new
science while preventing its serious impact on old institutional habits—including those of belief—that were
accepted as the foundation of norms and moral principles. In consequence the division would not stay put.
Upon the whole, without deliberate intent (though with
considerable deliberate encouragement from one group
of "advanced" philosophical thinkers) the consequences
issuing from the uses to which the new science was put
crowded in upon the activities and values nominally
reserved for the "spiritual." The impact of this en-
croachment constitutes what is called secularization, a

movement which, as it extended itself, was regarded as a sacrilegious profaning of the sacredness of the spiritual. Even today many men who are in no way practically identified with old ecclesiastical institutions, or with the metaphysics associated with it, speak regretfully and at best apologetically of this secularization. Yet the opportunity for any genuine universalization of the method—and spirit—of science as inquiry, which is perforce discovery in which old intellectual attitudes and conclusions are unceasingly yielding to the different and new, lies precisely in discovering how to give the factors of this secularization the shape, the content and the authority nominally assigned to morals, but not now exercised in fact by those morals that have come down to us from a pre-scientific age. The actuality of this loss of authority is acknowledged in the current revival of the old doctrine of the inherent depravity of human nature to account for the loss, as well as being shown in widespread pessimism as to the future of man. These complaints and doubts are warranted as long as one regards the institutional customs in action and belief of a pre-scientific age as ultimate and immutable. But they also apply, if they are employed that way, a challenge to develop a theory of morals that will give positive intellectual direction to man in developing the practical—that is, actually effective—morals which will utilize the resources now at our disposal to bring into

the activities and interests of human life order and
security, not only in place of confusion but on a wider
scale than ever existed in the past.

Three things are intimately connected in the plaints
and promulgations that are temporarily most vocal.
They are: (1) the attack upon natural science; (2) the
doctrine that man is so inherently corrupt that it is impossible to form morals which will operate in behalf of
stability, equity and (true) freedom without recourse
to an extra-human and extra-natural authority; and
(3) the claim put forth by representatives of some particular kind of institutional organization, that they
alone can do what is needed. I do not mention this
matter here in order to subject it to direct criticism.
I mention it because it presents a position so generalized
as clearly to indicate one direction in which philosophy
may move out of the apathy of irrelevance. By sharp
contrast, it points to the other direction in which philosophy may proceed: that of systematic endeavor to see
and to state the constructive significance for the future of man issuing from the revolution wrought primarily by the new science; provided we exercise resolute wisdom in developing a system of belief-attitudes,
a philosophy, framed on the basis of the resources now
at our command.

The issue actually raised by the assault upon the new
science and its offspring by wholesale condemnation of

human nature, and by the plea to reinstate in full measure the authority of antique medieval institutions, is simply whether we are to move forward in a direction made possible by these new resources or whether the latter are so inherently untrustworthy that we must bring them under control by subjection to an authority claiming to be extra-human and extra-natural—as far as the import of "natural" is determined by scientific inquiry. The impact of systematic perception of this cleavage of directions upon philosophy is disclosure that what is called "modern" is as yet unformed, inchoate. Its confused strife and its unstable uncertainties reflect the mixture of an old and a new that are incompatible. The genuinely modern has still to be brought into existence. The work of actual production is not the task or responsibility of philosophy. That work can be done only by the resolute, patient, co-operative activities of men and women of good will, drawn from every useful calling, over an indefinitely long period. There is no absurd claim made that philosophers, scientists or any other one group form a sacred priesthood to whom the work is entrusted. But, as philosophers in the last few centuries have performed a useful and needed work in furtherance of physical inquiry, so their successors now have the opportunity and the challenge to do a similar work in forwarding moral inquiry. The conclusions of that inquiry by themselves would no more constitute a complete moral theory and a working science of distinctively human subjectmatter than the activities of their predecessors brought the physical and physiological conditions of human existence into direct and full-fledged existence. But it would have an active share in the work of *con*struction of a moral human science which serves as a needful precursor of *re*construction of the actual state of human life toward order and toward other conditions of a fuller life than man has yet enjoyed.

Systematic exposure of how, where and why philosophies appropriate to ancient and medieval conditions and to those of the few centuries which have elapsed since the appearance of natural science on the human scene is so irrelevant as to be obstructive in intellectual dealings with the present scene, is itself a challenging intellectual task. As earlier intimated, reconstruction is not something to be accomplished by finding fault or being querulous. It is strictly an intellectual work demanding the widest possible scholarship as to the connections of past systems with the cultural conditions that set their problems and a knowledge of present-day science which is other than that of "popular" expositions. And this negative aspect of the intellectual activity to be performed involves of necessity a systematic exploration of the values belonging to what is genuinely new in the scientific, technological and political movements of the immediate past and of the present, when they are liberated from the incubus imposed on them by habits formed in a pre-scientific, pre-technological-industrial and pre-democratic political period.

One now fairly often runs across signs of a growing tendency to react against the view which holds that science and the new technology are to be blamed for present evils. It is recognized that as means they are so powerful as to give us valuable new resources. All that is needed, so it is held, is an equally effective moral renewal that will use these means for genuinely human ends. This position is certainly a marked improvement upon a mere assault on science and technology for the purpose of effecting a specific institutional subordination of them. It is to be welcomed in so far as it perceives that the matter at issue is moral or human. But—at least in the cases in which I have met it—it suffers from a serious defect. It appears to assume that we already have in our possession, ready-made, so to say, the morals that determine the ends for which the greatly enhanced store of means should be used. The *practical* difficulty in the way of rendering radically new "means" into servants of ends framed when the means at our disposal were of a different kind is ignored. But much more important than this, with respect to theory or philosophy, is the fact that it retains intact the divorce between some things as means and mere means and other things as ends and only ends because of their own essence or inherent nature. Thus in effect, though not in intent, an issue which is serious enough to be *moral* is disastrously evaded.

Just as this separation of some things as ends-in-themselves from other things as means-in-themselves, by their very nature, is a heritage of an age in which only those activities were called "useful" which served living physiologically rather than morally, and which were carried on by slaves or serfs to serve men who were *free* in the degree to which they were relieved from the need of labor that was base and material, so the primary need of the new state in which resources vastly different both qualitatively and quantitatively are at our command involves formation of new ends, ideals and standards to which to attach our new means. It is morally as well as logically impossible that a thoroughly changed kind of means should be harnessed to ends which at most are supposed to be changed only in the ease with which they can be reached. The thoroughgoing secularization of means and opportunities that has been going on has so far revolutionized the conduct of life as to have unsettled the old scene. Nothing is more intellectually futile (as well as practically impossible) than to suppose harmony and order can be achieved except as new ends and standards, new moral principles, are first developed with a reasonable degree of clarity and system.

In short, the problem of reconstruction in philosophy, from whatever angle it is approached, turns out to have its inception in the endeavor to discover how the new movements in science and in the industrial and political human conditions which have issued from it, that are as yet only inchoate and confused, shall be carried to completion. For a fulfillment which is consonant with their own, their proper, direction and momentum of movement can be achieved only in terms of ends and standards so distinctively human as to constitute a new moral order.

It is for the future to undertake, even in their philosophic aspect, the specific reconstructions that are involved in this carrying on to fulfillment what we have as yet attained only partially. Even a satisfactory listing of the issues that are involved with respect to philosophy must, by and large, wait till the philosophic movement in this direction has been carried beyond any point as yet attained. But one outstanding member of such a list has just received incidental attention: namely, the divorce that was set up between mere means and ends-in-themselves, which is the theoretical correlate of the sharp division of men into free and slave, superior and inferior. Science as conducted, science in practice, has completely repudiated these separations and isolations.

Scientific inquiry has raised activities, materials, tools, of the type once regarded as practical (in a low utilitarian sense) into itself; it has incorporated them into its own being. The way work is carried on in any astronomical observatory in the land, as well as in any physical laboratory, is evidence. Theory in formal statement also is as yet far behind theory in scientific practice. Theory in fact—that is, in the conduct of scientific inquiry—has lost ultimacy. Theories have passed into hypotheses. It remains for philosophy to point out in particular and in general the untold significance of this fact for morals. For in what is now taken to be morals the fixed, the immutable, still reign, even though moral theorists and moral institutional dogmatists are at complete odds with one another as to *what* ends, standards and principles are the ones which are immutable, eternal and universally applicable. In science the order of fixities has already passed irretrievably into an order of connections *in process*. One of the most immediate duties of philosophical reconstruction with respect to the development of viable instruments for inquiry into human or moral facts is to deal systematically with *human* processes.

Attention was earlier given in passing to some current misconceptions of the position set forth in the text which follows. I conclude with explicit notice of a point that has received repeated mention in the preceding text of the present Introduction. It has been charged that the view here taken of the work and subjectmatter of philosophy commits those who accept it to identification of philosophy with the work of those men called "reformers"—whether with praise or with disparagement. In a verbal sense re-form and re-construction are close together. But the re-construction or re-form here presented is strictly one of theory of the type that is so comprehensive in scope as to constitute philosophy. One of the operations to be undertaken in a re-constructed philosophy is to assemble and present reasons why the separation once set up between theory and practice no longer exists, so that a man like Justice Holmes can say that theory is the most practical thing, for good or for evil, in the world. One may hope surely that the theoretical enterprise herein presented will bear practical issue and for good. But that achievement is the work of human beings as human, not of them in any special professional capacity.

JOHN DEWEY

New York
October, 1948

PREFATORY NOTE

BEING invited to lecture at the Imperial University
of Japan in Tokyo during February and March of the
present year, I attempted an interpretation of the reconstruction of ideas and ways of thought now going on in
philosophy. While the lectures cannot avoid revealing
the marks of the particular standpoint of their author,
the aim is to exhibit the general contrasts between older
and newer types of philosophic problems rather than to
make a partisan plea in behalf of any one specific solution of these problems. I have tried for the most part
to set forth the forces which make intellectual reconstruction inevitable and to prefigure some of the lines
upon which it must proceed.

Any one who has enjoyed the unique hospitality of
Japan will be overwhelmed with confusion if he endeavors to make an acknowledgment in any way commensurate to the kindnesses he received. Yet I must
set down in the barest of black and white my grateful
appreciation of them, and in particular record my inef-
faceable impressions of the courtesy and help of the
members of the department of philosophy of Tokyo
University, and of my dear friends Dr. Ono and Dr.
Nitobe.   J. D.

September, 1919.

CONTENTS

RECONSTRUCTION IN PHILOSOPHY

CHAPTER I

CHANGING CONCEPTIONS OF PHILOSOPHY

MAN differs from the lower animals because he preserves his past experiences. What happened in the past is lived again in memory. About what goes on today hangs a cloud of thoughts concerning similar things undergone in bygone days. With the animals, an experience perishes as it happens, and each new doing or suffering stands alone. But man lives in a world where each occurrence is charged with echoes and reminiscences of what has gone before, where each event is a reminder of other things. Hence he lives not, like the beasts of the field, in a world of merely physical things but in a world of signs and symbols. A stone is not merely hard, a thing into which one bumps; but it is a monument of a deceased ancestor. A flame is not merely something which warms or burns, but is a symbol of the enduring life of the household, of the abiding source of cheer, nourishment and shelter to which man returns from his casual wanderings. Instead of being a quick fork of fire which may sting and hurt, it is the hearth at which one worships and for which one fights. And all this which marks the difference between bestiality and

1

humanity, between culture and merely physical nature, is because man remembers, preserving and recording his experiences.

The revivals of memory are, however, rarely literal. We naturally remember what interests us and because it interests us. The past is recalled not because of itself but because of what it adds to the present. Thus the primary life of memory is emotional rather than intellectual and practical. Savage man recalled yesterday's struggle with an animal not in order to study in a scientific way the qualities of the animal or for the sake of calculating how better to fight tomorrow, but to escape from the tedium of today by regaining the thrill of yesterday. The memory has all the excitement of the combat without its danger and anxiety. To revive it and revel in it is to enhance the present moment with a new meaning, a meaning different from that which actually belongs either to it or to the past. Memory is vicarious experience in which there is all the emotional values of actual experience without its strains, vicissitudes and troubles. The triumph of battle is even more poignant in the memorial war dance than at the moment of victory; the conscious and truly human experience of the chase comes when it is talked over and re-enacted by the camp fire. At the time, attention is taken up with practical details and with the strain of uncertainty. Only later do the details compose into a story and fuse into a whole of meaning. At the time of practical experience man exists from moment to moment, preoccupied with the task of the moment. As he resurveys all the moments in thought, a drama emerges with a beginning, a middle and a movement toward the climax of achievement or defeat.

Since man revives his past experience because of the interest added to what would otherwise be the emptiness of present leisure, the primitive life of memory is one of fancy and imagination, rather than of accurate recollection. After all, it is the story, the drama, which counts. Only those incidents are selected which have a present emotional value, to intensify the present tale as it is rehearsed in imagination or told to an admiring listener. What does not add to the thrill of combat or contribute to the goal of success or failure is dropped. Incidents are rearranged till they fit into the temper of the tale. Thus early man when left to himself, when not actually engaged in the struggle for existence, lived in a world of memories which was a world of suggestions. A suggestion differs from a recollection in that no attempt is made to test its correctness. Its correctness is a matter of relative indifference. The cloud suggests a camel or a man's face. It could not suggest these things unless some time there had been an actual, literal experience of camel and face. But the real likeness is of no account. The main thing is the emotional interest in tracing the camel or following the fortunes of the face as it forms and dissolves.

Students of the primitive history of mankind tell of the enormous part played by animal tales, myths and cults. Sometimes a mystery is made out of this historical fact, as if it indicated that primitive man was moved by a different psychology from that which now animates humanity. But the explanation is, I think, simple. Until agriculture and the higher industrial arts were developed, long periods of empty leisure alternated with comparatively short periods of energy put forth to secure food or safety from attack. Because of our own habits, we tend to think of people as busy or occupied, if not with doing at least with thinking and planning. But then men were busy only when engaged in the hunt or fishing or fighting expedition. Yet the mind when awake must have some filling; it cannot remain literally vacant because the body is idle. And what thoughts should crowd into the human mind except experiences with animals, experiences transformed under the influence of dramatic interest to make more vivid and coherent the events typical of the chase? As men in fancy dramatically re-lived the interesting parts of their actual lives, animals inevitably became themselves dramatized.

They were true *dramatis personæ* and as such assumed the traits of persons. They too had desires, hopes and fears, a life of affections, loves and hates, triumphs and defeats. Moreover, since they were essential to the support of the community, their activities and sufferings made them, in the imagination which dramatically revived the past, true sharers in the life of the community. Although they were hunted, yet they permitted themselves after all to be caught, and hence they were friends and allies. They devoted themselves, quite literally, to the sustenance and well-being of the community group to which they belonged. Thus were produced not merely the multitude of tales and legends dwelling affectionately upon the activities and features of animals, but also those elaborate rites and cults which made animals ancestors, heroes, tribal figure-heads and divinities.

I hope that I do not seem to you to have gone too far afield from my topic, the origin of philosophies. For it seems to me that the historic source of philosophies cannot be understood except as we dwell, at even greater length and in more detail, upon such considerations as these. We need to recognize that the ordinary consciousness of the ordinary man left to himself is a creature of desires rather than of intellectual study, inquiry or speculation. Man ceases to be primarily actuated by hopes and fears, loves and hates, only when he is subjected to a discipline which is foreign to human nature, which is, from the standpoint of natural man, artificial. Naturally our books, our scientific and philosophical books, are written by men who have subjected themselves in a superior degree to intellectual discipline and culture. Their thoughts are habitually reasonable. They have learned to check their fancies by facts, and to organize their ideas logically rather than emotionally and dramatically. When they do indulge in reverie and day-dreaming—which is probably more of the time than is conventionally acknowledged—they are aware of what they are doing. They label these excursions, and do not confuse their results with objective experiences. We tend to judge others by ourselves, and because scientific and philosophic books are composed by men in whom the reasonable, logical and objective habit of mind predominates, a similar rationality has been attributed by them to the average and ordinary man. It is then overlooked that both rationality and irrationality are largely irrelevant and episodical in undisciplined human nature; that men are governed by memory rather than by thought, and that memory is not a remembering of actual facts, but is association, suggestion, dramatic fancy. The standard used to measure the value of the suggestions that spring up in the mind is not congruity with fact but emotional congeniality. Do they stimulate and reinforce feeling, and fit into the dramatic tale? Are they consonant with the prevailing mood, and can they be rendered into the traditional hopes and fears of the community? If we are willing to take the word dreams with a certain liberality, it is hardly too much to say that man, save in his occasional times of actual work and struggle, lives in a world of dreams, rather than of facts, and a world of dreams that is organized about desires whose success and frustration form its stuff.

To treat the early beliefs and traditions of mankind as if they were attempts at scientific explanation of the world, only erroneous and absurd attempts, is thus to be guilty of a great mistake. The material out of which philosophy finally emerges is irrelevant to science and to explanation. It is figurative, symbolic of fears and hopes, made of imaginations and suggestions, not significant of a world of objective fact intellectually confronted. It is poetry and drama, rather than science, and is apart from scientific truth and falsity, rationality or absurdity of fact in the same way in which poetry is independent of these things.

This original material has, however, to pass through at least two stages before it becomes philosophy proper. One is the stage in which stories and legends and their accompanying dramatizations are consolidated. At first the emotionalized records of experiences are largely casual and transitory. Events that excite the emotions of an individual are seized upon and lived over in tale and pantomime. But some experiences are so frequent and recurrent that they concern the group as a whole. They are socially generalized. The piecemeal adventure of the single individual is built out till it becomes representative and typical of the emotional life of the tribe. Certain incidents affect the weal and woe of the group in its entirety and thereby get an exceptional emphasis and elevation. A certain texture of tradition is built up; the story becomes a social heritage and possession; the pantomime develops into the stated rite. Tradition thus formed becomes a kind of norm to which individual fancy and suggestion conform. An abiding framework of imagination is constructed. A communal way of conceiving life grows up into which individuals are inducted by education. Both unconsciously and by definite social requirement individual memories are assimilated to group memory or tradition, and individual fancies are accommodated to the body of beliefs characteristic of a community. Poetry becomes fixated and systematized. The story becomes a social norm. The original drama which re-enacts an emotionally important experience is institutionalized into a cult. Suggestions previously free are hardened into doctrines.

The systematic and obligatory nature of such doctrines is hastened and confirmed through conquests and political consolidation. As the area of a government is extended, there is a definite motive for systematizing and unifying beliefs once free and floating. Aside from natural accommodation and assimilation springing from the fact of intercourse and the needs of common understanding, there is often political necessity which leads the ruler to centralize traditions and beliefs in order to extend and strengthen his prestige and authority. Judea, Greece, Rome, and I presume all other countries having a long history, present records of a continual working over of earlier local rites and doctrines in the interests of a wider social unity and a more extensive political power. I shall ask you to assume with me that in this way the larger cosmogonies and cosmologies of the race as well as the larger ethical traditions have arisen. Whether this is literally so or not, it is not necessary to inquire, much less to demonstrate. It is enough for our purposes that under social influences there took place a fixing and organizing of doctrines and cults which gave general traits to the imagination and general rules to conduct, and that such a consolidation was a necessary antecedent to the formation of any philosophy as we understand that term.

Although a necessary antecedent, this organization and generalization of ideas and principles of belief is not the sole and sufficient generator of philosophy. There is still lacking the motive for logical system and intellectual proof. This we may suppose to be furnished by the need of reconciling the moral rules and ideals embodied in the traditional code with the matter of fact positivistic knowledge which gradually grows up. For man can never be wholly the creature of suggestion and fancy. The requirements of continued existence make indispensable some attention to the actual facts of the world. Although it is surprising how little check the environment actually puts upon the formation of ideas, since no notions are too absurd not to have been accepted by some people, yet the environment does enforce a certain minimum of correctness under penalty of extinction. That certain things are foods, that they are to be found in certain places, that water drowns, fire burns, that sharp points penetrate and cut, that heavy things fall unless supported, that there is a certain regularity in the changes of day and night and the alternation of hot and cold, wet and dry:—such prosaic facts force themselves upon even primitive attention. Some of them are so obvious and so important that they have next to no fanciful context. Auguste Comte says somewhere that he knows of no savage people who had a God of weight although every other natural quality or force may have been deified. Gradually there grows up a body of homely generalizations preserving and transmitting the wisdom of the race about the observed facts and sequences of nature. This knowledge is especially connected with industries, arts and crafts where observation of materials and processes is required for successful action, and where action is so continuous and regular that spasmodic magic will not suffice. Extravagantly fantastic notions are eliminated because they are brought into juxtaposition with what actually happens.

The sailor is more likely to be given to what we now term superstitions than say the weaver, because his activity is more at the mercy of sudden change and unforeseen occurrence. But even the sailor while he may regard the wind as the uncontrollable expression of the caprice of a great spirit, will still have to become acquainted with some purely mechanical principles of adjustment of boat, sails and oar to the wind. Fire may be conceived as a supernatural dragon because some time or other a swift, bright and devouring flame called before the mind's eye the quick-moving and dangerous serpent. But the housewife who tends the fire and the pots wherein food cooks will still be compelled to observe certain mechanical facts of draft and replenishment, and passage from wood to ash. Still more will the worker in metals accumulate verifiable details about the conditions and consequences of the operation of heat. He may retain for special and ceremonial occasions traditional beliefs, but everyday familiar use will expel these conceptions for the greater part of the time, when fire will be to him of uniform and prosaic behavior, controllable by practical relations of cause and effect.

As the arts and crafts develop and become more elaborate, the body of positive and tested knowledge enlarges,
and the sequences observed become more complex and of
greater scope.   Technologies of this kind give that
common-sense knowledge of nature out of which science
takes its origin.   They provide not merely a collection
of positive facts, but they give expertness in dealing
with materials and tools, and promote the development
of the experimental habit of mind, as soon as an art
can be taken away from the rule of sheer custom.

For a long time the imaginative body of beliefs closely
connected with the moral habits of a community group
and with its emotional indulgences and consolations per-
sists side by side with the growing body of matter of
fact knowledge.   Wherever possible they are interlaced.
At other points, their inconsistencies forbid their inter-
weaving, but the two things are kept apart as if in
different compartments.   Since one is merely super-
imposed upon the other their incompatibility is not felt,
and there is no need of reconciliation.   In most cases,
the two kinds of mental products are kept apart because
they become the possession of separate social classes.
The religious and poetic beliefs having acquired a definite social and political value and function are in the
keeping of a higher class directly associated with the
ruling elements in the society.   The workers and crafts-
men who possess the prosaic matter of fact knowledge

are likely to occupy a low social status, and their kind of knowledge is affected by the social disesteem entertained for the manual worker who engages in activities useful to the body. It doubtless was this fact in Greece which in spite of the keenness of observation, the extraordinary power of logical reasoning and the great freedom of speculation attained by the Athenian, postponed the general and systematic employment of the experimental method. Since the industrial craftsman was only just above the slave in social rank, his type of knowledge and the method upon which it depended lacked prestige and authority.

Nevertheless, the time came when matter of fact knowledge increased to such bulk and scope that it came into conflict with not merely the detail but with the spirit and temper of traditional and imaginative beliefs. Without going into the vexed question of how and why, there is no doubt that this is just what happened in what we term the sophistic movement in Greece, within which originated philosophy proper in the sense in which the western world understands that term. The fact that the sophists had a bad name given them by Plato and Aristotle, a name they have never been able to shake off, is evidence that with the sophists the strife between the two types of belief was the emphatic thing, and that the conflict had a disconcerting effect upon the traditional system of religious beliefs and the moral code of conduct bound up with it. Although Socrates was doubtless sincerely interested in the reconciliation of the two sides, yet the fact that he approached the matter from the side of matter of fact method, giving its canons and criteria primacy, was enough to bring him to the condemnation of death as a contemner of the gods and a corrupter of youth.

The fate of Socrates and the ill-fame of the sophists may be used to suggest some of the striking contrasts between traditional emotionalized belief on one hand and prosaic matter of fact knowledge on the other:— the purpose of the comparison being to bring out the point that while all the advantages of what we call science were on the side of the latter, the advantages of social esteem and authority, and of intimate contact with what gives life its deeper lying values were on the side of traditional belief. To all appearances, the specific and verified knowledge of the environment had only a limited and technical scope. It had to do with the arts, and the purpose and good of the artisan after all did not extend very far. They were subordinate and almost servile. Who would put the art of the shoemaker on the same plane as the art of ruling the state? Who would put even the higher art of the physician in healing the body, upon the level of the art of the priest in healing the soul? Thus Plato constantly draws the contrast in his dialogues. The shoemaker is a judge of a good pair of shoes, but he is no judge at all of the more important question whether and when it is good to wear shoes; the physician is a good judge of health, but whether it is a good thing or not to be well or better to die, he knows not. While the artisan is expert as long as purely limited technical questions arise, he is helpless when it comes to the only really important questions, the moral questions as to values. Consequently, his type of knowledge is inherently inferior and needs to be controlled by a higher kind of knowledge which will reveal ultimate ends and purposes, and thus put and keep technical and mechanical knowledge in its proper place. Moreover, in Plato's pages we find, because of Plato's adequate dramatic sense, a lively depicting of the impact in particular men of the conflict between tradition and the new claims of purely intellectual knowledge. The conservative is shocked beyond measure at the idea of teaching the military art by abstract rules, by science. One does not just fight, one fights for one's country. Abstract science cannot convey love and loyalty, nor can it be a substitute, even upon the more technical side, for those ways and means of fighting in which devotion to the country has been traditionally embodied.

The way to learn the fighting art is through association with those who have themselves learned to defend the country, by becoming saturated with its ideals and customs; by becoming in short a practical adept in the Greek tradition as to fighting. To attempt to derive abstract rules from a comparison of native ways of fighting with the enemies' ways is to begin to go over to the enemies' traditions and gods: it is to begin to be false to one's own country.

Such a point of view vividly realized enables us to appreciate the antagonism aroused by the positivistic point of view when it came into conflict with the traditional. The latter was deeply rooted in social habits and loyalties; it was surcharged with the moral aims for which men lived and the moral rules by which they lived. Hence it was as basic and as comprehensive as life itself, and palpitated with the warm glowing colors of the community life in which men realized their own being. In contrast, the positivistic knowledge was concerned with merely physical utilities, and lacked the ardent associations of belief hallowed by sacrifices of ancestors and worship of contemporaries. Because of its limited and concrete character it was dry, hard, cold.

Yet the more acute and active minds, like that of Plato himself, could no longer be content to accept, along with the conservative citizen of the time, the old beliefs in the old way. The growth of positive knowledge and of the critical, inquiring spirit undermined these in their old form. The advantages in definiteness, in accuracy, in verifiability were all on the side of the new knowledge. Tradition was noble in aim and scope, but uncertain in foundation. The unquestioned life, said Socrates, was not one fit to be lived by man, who is a questioning being because he is a rational being. Hence he must search out the reason of things, and not accept them from custom and political authority. What was to be done? Develop a method of rational investigation and proof which should place the essential elements of traditional belief upon an unshakable basis; develop a method of thought and knowledge which while purifying tradition should preserve its moral and social values unimpaired; nay, by purifying them, add to their power and authority. To put it in a word, that which had rested upon custom was to be restored, resting no longer upon the habits of the past, but upon the very metaphysics of Being and the Universe. Metaphysics is a substitute for custom as the source and guarantor of higher moral and social values—that is the leading theme of the classic philosophy of Europe, as evolved by Plato and Aristotle—a philosophy, let us always recall, renewed and restated by the Christian philosophy of Medieval Europe.

Out of this situation emerged, if I mistake not, the entire tradition regarding the function and office of philosophy which till very recently has controlled the systematic and constructive philosophies of the western world. If I am right in my main thesis that the origin of philosophy lay in an attempt to reconcile the two different types of mental product, then the key is in our hands as to the main traits of subsequent philosophy so far as that was not of a negative and heterodox kind. In the first place, philosophy did not develop in an unbiased way from an open and unprejudiced origin. It had its task cut out for it from the start. It had a mission to perform, and it was sworn in advance to that mission. It had to extract the essential moral kernel out of the threatened traditional beliefs of the past. So far so good; the work was critical and in the interests of the only true conservatism—that which will conserve and not waste the values wrought out by humanity. But it was also precommitted to extracting this moral essence in a spirit congenial to the spirit of past beliefs. The association with imagination and with social authority was too intimate to be deeply disturbed. It was not possible to conceive of the content of social institutions in any form radically different from that in which they had existed in the past. It became the work of philosophy to justify on rational grounds the spirit, though not the form, of accepted beliefs and traditional customs.

The resulting philosophy seemed radical enough and

even dangerous to the average Athenian because of the
difference of form and method.   In the sense of pruning
away excrescences and eliminating factors which to the
average citizen were all one with the basic beliefs, it
was radical.   But looked at in the perspective of history
and in contrast with different types of thought which
developed later in different social environments, it is
now easy to see how profoundly, after all, Plato and
Aristotle reflected the meaning of Greek tradition and
habit, so that their writings remain, with the writings
of the great dramatists, the best introduction of a student into the innermost ideals and aspirations of distinctively Greek life.   Without Greek religion, Greek
art, Greek civic life, their philosophy would have been
impossible; while the effect of that science upon which
the philosophers most prided themselves turns out to
have been superficial and negligible.   This apologetic
spirit of philosophy is even more apparent when Medieval Christianity about the twelfth century sought for a
systematic rational presentation of itself and made
use of classic philosophy, especially that of Aristotle, to
justify itself to reason.   A not unsimilar occurrence
characterizes the chief philosophic systems of Germany
in the early nineteenth century, when Hegel assumed the
task of justifying in the name of rational idealism the
doctrines and institutions which were menaced by the
new spirit of science and popular government.   The

result has been that the great systems have not been free from party spirit exercised in behalf of pre-conceived beliefs. Since they have at the same time professed complete intellectual independence and rationality, the result has been too often to impart to philosophy an element of insincerity, all the more insidious because wholly unconscious on the part of those who sustained philosophy.

And this brings us to a second trait of philosophy springing from its origin. Since it aimed at a rational justification of things that had been previously accepted because of their emotional congeniality and social prestige, it had to make much of the apparatus of reason and proof. Because of the lack of intrinsic rationality in the matters with which it dealt, it leaned over backward, so to speak, in parade of logical form. In dealing with matters of fact, simpler and rougher ways of demonstration may be resorted to. It is enough, so to say, to produce the fact in question and point to it—the fundamental form of all demonstration. But when it comes to convincing men of the truth of doctrines which are no longer to be accepted upon the say-so of custom and social authority, but which also are not capable of empirical verification, there is no recourse save to magnify the signs of rigorous thought and rigid demonstration. Thus arises that appearance of abstract definition and ultra-scientific argumentation which repels so many from philosophy but which has been one of its chief attractions to its devotees.

At the worst, this has reduced philosophy to a show of elaborate terminology, a hair-splitting logic, and a fictitious devotion to the mere external forms of comprehensive and minute demonstration. Even at the best, it has tended to produce an overdeveloped attachment to system for its own sake, and an over-pretentious claim to certainty. Bishop Butler declared that probability is the guide of life; but few philosophers have been courageous enough to avow that philosophy can be satisfied with anything that is merely probable. The customs dictated by tradition and desire had claimed finality and immutability. They had claimed to give certain and unvarying laws of conduct. Very early in its history philosophy made pretension to a similar conclusiveness, and something of this temper has clung to classic philosophies ever since. They have insisted that they were more scientific than the sciences—that, indeed, philosophy was necessary because after all the special sciences fail in attaining final and complete truth. There have been a few dissenters who have ventured to assert, as did William James, that " philosophy is vision " and that its chief function is to free men's minds from bias and prejudice and to enlarge their perceptions of the world about them. But in the main philosophy has set up much more ambitious pretensions.

To say frankly that philosophy can proffer nothing but hypotheses, and that these hypotheses are of value only as they render men's minds more sensitive to life about them, would seem like a negation of philosophy itself.

In the third place, the body of beliefs dictated by desire and imagination and developed under the influence of communal authority into an authoritative tradition, was pervasive and comprehensive. It was, so to speak, omnipresent in all the details of the group life. Its pressure was unremitting and its influence universal. It was then probably inevitable that the rival principle, reflective thought, should aim at a similar universality and comprehensiveness. It would be as inclusive and far-reaching metaphysically as tradition had been socially. Now there was just one way in which this pretension could be accomplished in conjunction with a claim of complete logical system and certainty.

All philosophies of the classic type have made a fixed and fundamental distinction between two realms of existence. One of these corresponds to the religious and supernatural world of popular tradition, which in its metaphysical rendering became the world of highest and ultimate reality. Since the final source and sanction of all important truths and rules of conduct in community life had been found in superior and unquestioned religious beliefs, so the absolute and supreme reality of philosophy afforded the only sure guaranty of truth about empirical matters, and the sole rational guide to proper social institutions and individual behavior. Over against this absolute and noumenal reality which could be apprehended only by the systematic discipline of philosophy itself stood the ordinary empirical, relatively real, phenomenal world of everyday experience. It was with this world that the practical affairs and utilities of men were connected. It was to this imperfect and perishing world that matter of fact, positivistic science referred.

This is the trait which, in my opinion, has affected most deeply the classic notion about the nature of philosophy. Philosophy has arrogated to itself the office of demonstrating the existence of a transcendent, absolute or inner reality and of revealing to man the nature and features of this ultimate and higher reality. It has therefore claimed that it was in possession of a higher organ of knowledge than is employed by positive science and ordinary practical experience, and that it is marked by a superior dignity and importance—a claim which is undeniable *if* philosophy leads man to proof and intuition of a Reality beyond that open to day-by-day life and the special sciences.

This claim has, of course, been denied by various

philosophers from time to time. But for the most part these denials have been agnostic and sceptical. They have contented themselves with asserting that absolute and ultimate reality is beyond human ken. But they have not ventured to deny that such Reality would be the appropriate sphere for the exercise of philosophic knowledge provided only it were within the reach of human intelligence. Only comparatively recently has another conception of the proper office of philosophy arisen. This course of lectures will be devoted to setting forth this different conception of philosophy in some of its main contrasts to what this lecture has termed the classic conception. At this point, it can be referred to only by anticipation and in cursory fashion. It is implied in the account which has been given of the origin of philosophy out of the background of an authoritative tradition; a tradition originally dictated by man's imagination working under the influence of love and hate and in the interest of emotional excitement and satisfaction. Common frankness requires that it be stated that this account of the origin of philosophies claiming to deal with absolute Being in a systematic way has been given with malice prepense. It seems to me that this genetic method of approach is a more effective way of undermining this type of philosophic theorizing than any attempt at logical refutation could be.

If this lecture succeeds in leaving in your minds as a reasonable hypothesis the idea that philosophy originated not out of intellectual material, but out of social and emotional material, it will also succeed in leaving with you a changed attitude toward traditional philosophies. They will be viewed from a new angle and placed in a new light. New questions about them will be aroused and new standards for judging them will be suggested.

If any one will commence without mental reservations to study the history of philosophy not as an isolated thing but as a chapter in the development of civilization and culture; if one will connect the story of philosophy with a study of anthropology, primitive life, the history of religion, literature and social institutions, it is confidently asserted that he will reach his own independent judgment as to the worth of the account which has been presented today. Considered in this way, the history of philosophy will take on a new significance. What is lost from the standpoint of would-be science is regained from the standpoint of humanity. Instead of the disputes of rivals about the nature of reality, we have the scene of human clash of social purpose and aspirations. Instead of impossible attempts to transcend experience, we have the significant record of the efforts of men to formulate the things of experience to which they are most deeply and passionately attached.

Instead of impersonal and purely speculative endeavors to contemplate as remote beholders the nature of absolute things-in-themselves, we have a living picture of the choice of thoughtful men about what they would have life to be, and to what ends they would have men shape their intelligent activities.

Any one of you who arrives at such a view of past philosophy will of necessity be led to entertain a quite definite conception of the scope and aim of future philosophizing. He will inevitably be committed to the notion that what philosophy has been unconsciously, without knowing or intending it, and, so to speak, under cover, it must henceforth be openly and deliberately. When it is acknowledged that under disguise of dealing with ultimate reality, philosophy has been occupied with the precious values embedded in social traditions, that it has sprung from a clash of social ends and from a conflict of inherited institutions with incompatible contemporary tendencies, it will be seen that the task of future philosophy is to clarify men's ideas as to the social and moral strifes of their own day. Its aim is to become so far as is humanly possible an organ for dealing with these conflicts. That which may be pretentiously unreal when it is formulated in metaphysical distinctions becomes intensely significant when connected with the drama of the struggle of social beliefs and ideals. Philosophy which surrenders its somewhat

barren monopoly of dealings with Ultimate and Absolute Reality will find a compensation in enlightening
the moral forces which move mankind and in contributing to the aspirations of men to attain to a more ordered
and intelligent happiness.

CHAPTER II

SOME HISTORICAL FACTORS IN PHILOSOPHI- CAL RECONSTRUCTION

FRANCIS BACON of the Elizabethan age is the great forerunner of the spirit of modern life. Though slight in accomplishment, as a prophet of new tendencies he is an outstanding figure of the world's intellectual life. Like many another prophet he suffers from confused intermingling of old and new. What is most significant in him has been rendered more or less familiar by the later course of events. But page after page is filled with matter which belongs to the past from which Bacon thought he had escaped. Caught between these two sources of easy disparagement, Bacon hardly receives his due as the real founder of modern thought, while he is praised for merits which scarcely belong to him, such as an alleged authorship of the specific methods of induction pursued by science. What makes Bacon memorable is that breezes blowing from a new world caught and filled his sails and stirred him to adventure in new seas. He never himself discovered the land of promise, but he proclaimed the new goal and by faith he descried its features from afar.

The main traits of his thought put before our mind
the larger features of a new spirit which was at work in
causing intellectual reconstruction. They may suggest
the social and historical forces out of which the new
spirit was born. The best known aphorism of Bacon
is that Knowledge is Power. Judged by this pragmatic
criterion, he condemned the great body of learning then
extant as *not*-knowledge, as pseudo- and pretentious-
knowledge. For it did not give power. It was otiose,
not operative. In his most extensive discussion he
classified the learning of his day under three heads,
delicate, fantastic and contentious. Under delicate
learning, he included the literary learning which through
the influence of the revival of ancient languages and
literatures occupied so important a place in the intellectual life of the Renaissance. Bacon's condemnation is
the more effective because he himself was a master of
the classics and of all the graces and refinements which
this literary study was intended to convey. In substance he anticipated most of the attacks which educa-
tional reformers since his time have made upon one-
sided literary culture. It contributed not to power but
to ornament and decoration. It was ostentatious and
luxurious. By fantastic learning he meant the quasi-
magical science that was so rife all over Europe in the
sixteenth century—wild developments of alchemy,
astrology, etc. Upon this he poured his greatest vials

of wrath because the corruption of the good is the worst of evils. Delicate learning was idle and vain, but fantastic learning aped the form of true knowledge. It laid hold of the true principle and aim of knowledge— control of natural forces. But it neglected the conditions and methods by which alone such knowledge could be obtained, and thus deliberately led men astray.

For our purposes, however, what he says about contentious learning is the most important. For by this, he means the traditional science which had come down, in scanty and distorted measure to be sure, from antiquity through scholasticism. It is called contentious both because of the logical method used and the end to which it was put. In a certain sense it aimed at power, but power over other men in the interest of some class or sect or person, not power over natural forces in the common interest of all. Bacon's conviction of the quarrelsome, self-displaying character of the scholarship which had come down from antiquity was of course not so much due to Greek science itself as to the degenerate heritage of scholasticism in the fourteenth century, when philosophy had fallen into the hands of disputatious theologians, full of hair-splitting argumentativeness and quirks and tricks by which to win victory over somebody else.

But Bacon also brought his charge against the Aristotelian method itself. In its rigorous forms it aimed at demonstration, and in its milder forms at persuasion. But both demonstration and persuasion aim at conquest of mind rather than of nature. Moreover they both assume that some one is already in possession of a truth or a belief, and that the only problem is to convince some one else, or to teach. In contrast, his new method had an exceedingly slight opinion of the amount of truth already existent, and a lively sense of the extent and importance of truths still to be attained. It would be a logic of discovery, not a logic of argumentation, proof and persuasion. To Bacon, the old logic even at its best was a logic for teaching the already known, and teaching meant indoctrination, discipling. It was an axiom of Aristotle that only that which was already known could be learned, that growth in knowledge consisted simply in bringing together a universal truth of reason and a particular truth of sense which had previously been noted separately. In any case, learning meant *growth* of knowledge, and growth belongs in the region of becoming, change, and hence is inferior to *possession* of knowledge in the syllogistic self-revolving manipulation of what was already known —demonstration.

In contrast with this point of view, Bacon eloquently proclaimed the superiority of discovery of new facts and truths to demonstration of the old. Now there is only one road to discovery, and that is penetrating in-

quiry into the secrets of nature. Scientific principles
and laws do not lie on the surface of nature. They are
hidden, and must be wrested from nature by an active
and elaborate technique of inquiry. Neither logical
reasoning nor the passive accumulation of any number
of observations—which the ancients called experience—
suffices to lay hold of them. Active experimentation
must force the apparent facts of nature into forms
different to those in which they familiarly present themselves; and thus make them tell the truth about themselves, as torture may compel an unwilling witness to reveal what he has been concealing. Pure reasoning as a
means of arriving at truth is like the spider who spins
a web out of himself. The web is orderly and elaborate,
but it is only a trap. The passive accumulation of
experiences—the traditional empirical method—is like
the ant who busily runs about and collects and piles up
heaps of raw materials. True method, that which Bacon
would usher in, is comparable to the operations of the
bee who, like the ant, collects material from the external
world, but unlike that industrious creature attacks and
modifies the collected stuff in order to make it yield its
hidden treasure.

Along with this contrast between subjugation of nature and subjection of other minds and the elevation
of a method of discovery above a method of demonstration, went Bacon's sense of progress as the aim and

test of genuine knowledge. According to his criticisms,
the classic logic, even in its Aristotelian form, inevitably
played into the hands of inert conservatism. For in
accustoming the mind to think of truth as already
known, it habituated men to fall back on the intellectual
attainments of the past, and to accept them without
critical scrutiny. Not merely the medieval but the
renaissance mind tended to look back to antiquity as a
Golden Age of Knowledge, the former relying upon
sacred scriptures, the latter upon secular literatures.
And while this attitude could not fairly be charged up
against the classic logic, yet Bacon felt, and with
justice, that any logic which identified the technique
of knowing with demonstration of truths already possessed by the mind, blunts the spirit of investigation and
confines the mind within the circle of traditional learning.

Such a logic could not avoid having for its salient
features definition of what is already known (or thought
to be known), and its systematization according to
recognized canons of orthodoxy. A logic of discovery
on the other hand looks to the future. Received truth
it regards critically as something to be tested by new
experiences rather than as something to be dogmatically
taught and obediently received. Its chief interest in
even the most carefully tested ready-made knowledge
is the use which may be made of it in further inquiries

and discoveries. Old truth has its chief value in assist-
ing the detection of new truth. Bacon's own appreciation of the nature of induction was highly defective.
But his acute sense that science means invasion of the
unknown, rather than repetition in logical form of the
already known, makes him nevertheless the father of
induction. Endless and persistent uncovering of facts
and principles not known—such is the true spirit of
induction. Continued progress in knowledge is the only
sure way of protecting old knowledge from degeneration
into dogmatic doctrines received on authority, or from
imperceptible decay into superstition and old wives'
tales.

Ever-renewed progress is to Bacon the test as well
as the aim of genuine logic. Where, Bacon constantly
demands, where are the works, the fruits, of the older
logic? What has it done to ameliorate the evils of life,
to rectify defects, to improve conditions? Where are
the inventions that justify its claim to be in possession
of truth? Beyond the victory of man over man in
law courts, diplomacy and political administration,
they are nil. One had to turn from admired " sciences "
to despised arts to find works, fruits, consequences of
value to human kind through power over natural forces.
And progress in the arts was as yet intermittent, fitful,
accidental. A true logic or technique of inquiry would
make advance in the industrial, agricultural and medi-

cal arts continuous, cumulative and deliberately systematic.

If we take into account the supposed body of ready-
made knowledge upon which learned men rested in
supine acquiescence and which they recited in parrot-
like chorus, we find it consists of two parts. One
of these parts is made up of the errors of our ancestors, musty with antiquity and organized into pseudo-
science through the use of the classic logic. Such
" truths " are in fact only the systematized mistakes
and prejudices of our ancestors. Many of them originated in accident; many in class interest and bias, perpetuated by authority for this very reason—a consideration which later actuated Locke's attack upon the
doctrine of innate ideas. The other portion of accepted
beliefs comes from instinctive tendencies of the human
mind that give it a dangerous bias until counteracted
by a conscious and critical logic.

The mind of man spontaneously assumes greater simplicity, uniformity and unity among phenomena than
actually exists. It follows superficial analogies and
jumps to conclusions; it overlooks the variety of details and the existence of exceptions. Thus it weaves a
web of purely internal origin which it imposes upon
nature. What had been termed science in the past consisted of this humanly constructed and imposed web.
Men looked at the work of their own minds and thought

they were seeing realities in nature. They were wor-
shipping, under the name of science, the idols of their
own making. So-called science and philosophy consisted of these " anticipations " of nature. And the
worst thing that could be said about traditional logic
was that instead of saving man from this natural source
of error, it had, though attributing to nature a false
rationality of unity, simplicity and generality, sanctioned these sources of delusion. The office of the new
logic would be to protect the mind against itself: to
teach it to undergo a patient and prolonged appren-
ticeship to fact in its infinite variety and particularity:
to obey nature intellectually in order to command it
practically. Such was the significance of the new logic
—the new tool or organon of learning, so named in
express opposition to the organon of Aristotle.

Certain other important oppositions are implied.
Aristotle thought of reason as capable of solitary com-
munion with rational truth. The counterpart of his
celebrated saying that man is a political animal, is that
Intelligence, *Nous*, is neither animal, human nor political. It is divinely unique and self-enclosed. To Bacon,
error had been produced and perpetuated by social influences, and truth must be discovered by social agencies
organized for that purpose. Left to himself, the individual can do little or nothing; he is likely to become
involved in his own self-spun web of misconceptions.

The great need is the organization of co-operative research, whereby men attack nature collectively and the work of inquiry is carried on continuously from generation to generation. Bacon even aspired to the rather absurd notion of a method so perfected that differences in natural human ability might be discounted, and all be put on the same level in production of new facts and new truths. Yet this absurdity was only the negative side of his great positive prophecy of a combined and co-operative pursuit of science such as characterizes our own day. In view of the picture he draws in his New Atlantis of a State organized for collective inquiry, we readily forgive him his exaggerations.

Power over nature was not to be individual but collective; the Empire, as he says, of Man over Nature, substituted for the Empire of Man over Man. Let us employ Bacon's own words with their variety of picturesque metaphor: " Men have entered into the desire of learning and knowledge, . . . seldom sincerely to give a true account of their gift of reason, to the benefit and use of men, but as if they sought in knowledge a couch whereon to rest a searching and wandering spirit; or a terrace for a wandering and variable mind to walk up and down with a fair prospect; or a tower for a proud mind to raise itself upon; or a fort or commanding ground for strife and contention; or a shop for profit and sale; and not a rich storehouse for the glory of the creator and the relief of man's estate." When William James called Pragmatism a New Name for an Old Way of Thinking, I do not know that he was thinking expressly of Francis Bacon, but so far as concerns the spirit and atmosphere of the pursuit of knowledge, Bacon may be taken as the prophet of a pragmatic conception of knowledge. Many misconceptions of its spirit would be avoided if his emphasis upon the social factor in both the pursuit and the end of knowledge were carefully observed.

This somewhat over-long résumé of Bacon's ideas has not been gone into as a matter of historic retrospect. The summary is rather meant to put before our minds an authentic document of the new philosophy which may bring into relief the social causes of intellectual revolution. Only a sketchy account can be here attempted, but it may be of some assistance even barely to remind you of the direction of that industrial, political and religious change upon which Europe was entering.

Upon the industrial side, it is impossible, I think, to exaggerate the influence of travel, exploration and new commerce which fostered a romantic sense of adventure into novelty; loosened the hold of traditional beliefs; created a lively sense of new worlds to be investigated and subdued; produced new methods of manufacture, commerce, banking and finance; and then reacted everywhere to stimulate invention, and to intro-

duce positive observation and active experimentation
into science. The Crusades, the revival of the profane
learning of antiquity and even more perhaps, the contact with the advanced learning of the Mohammedans,
the increase of commerce with Asia and Africa, the
introduction of the lens, compass and gunpowder, the
finding and opening up of North and South America—
most significantly called The New World—these are
some of the obvious external facts. Contrast between
peoples and races previously isolated is always, I think,
most fruitful and influential for change when psychological and industrial changes coincide with and reinforce each other. Sometimes people undergo emotional
change, what might almost be called a metaphysical
change, through intercourse. The inner set of the mind,
especially in religious matters, is altered. At other
times, there is a lively exchange of goods, an adoption
of foreign tools and devices, an imitation of alien habits
of clothing, habitation and production of commodities.
One of these changes is, so to speak, too internal and the
other too external to bring about a profound intellectual
development. But when the creation of a new mental
attitude falls together with extensive material and
economic changes, something significant happens.

This coincidence of two kinds of change was, I take it,
characteristic of the new contacts of the sixteenth and
seventeenth centuries. Clash of customs and traditional

beliefs dispelled mental inertia and sluggishness; it
aroused a lively curiosity as to different and new ideas.
The actual adventure of travel and exploration purged
the mind of fear of the strange and unknown: as new
territories geographically and commercially speaking
were opened up, the mind was opened up. New contacts
promoted the desire for still more contacts; the appetite
for novelty and discovery grew by what it fed upon.
Conservative adherence to old beliefs and methods
underwent a steady attrition with every new voyage
into new parts and every new report of foreign ways.
The mind became used to exploration and discovery. It
found a delight and interest in the revelations of the
novel and the unusual which it no longer took in what
was old and customary. Moreover, the very act of
exploration, of expedition, the process of enterprising
adventure into the remote, yielded a peculiar joy and
thrill.

This psychological change was essential to the birth
of the new point of view in science and philosophy.
Yet alone it could hardly have produced the new method
of knowing. But positive changes in the habits and
purposes of life gave objective conformation and support to the mental change. They also determined the
channels in which the new spirit found exercise. New-
found wealth, the gold from the Americas and new articles of consumption and enjoyment, tended to wean men

from preoccupation with the metaphysical and theological, and to turn their minds with newly awakened interest to the joys of nature and this life. New material resources and new markets in America and India undermined the old dependence upon household and manual production for a local and limited market, and generated quantitative, large scale production by means of steam for foreign and expanding markets. Capitalism, rapid transit, and production for exchange against money and for profit, instead of against goods and for consumption, followed.

This cursory and superficial reminder of vast and complicated events may suggest the mutual interdependence of the scientific revolution and the industrial revolution. Upon the one hand, modern industry *is* so much applied science. No amount of desire to make money, or to enjoy new commodities, no amount of mere practical energy and enterprise, would have effected the economic transformation of the last few centuries and generations. Improvements in mathematical, physical, chemical and biological science were prerequisites. Business men through engineers of different sorts, have laid hold of the new insights gained by scientific men into the hidden energies of nature, and have turned them to account. The modern mine, factory, railway, steamship, telegraph, all of the appliances and equipment of production, and transportation, express scientific knowledge. They would continue unimpaired even if the ordinary pecuniary accompaniments of economic activity were radically altered. In short, through the intermediary of invention, Bacon's watchword that knowledge is power and his dream of continuous empire over natural forces by means of natural science have been actualized. The industrial revolution by steam and electricity is the reply to Bacon's prophecy.

On the other hand, it is equally true that the needs of modern industry have been tremendous stimuli to scientific investigation. The demands of progressive production and transportation have set new problems to inquiry; the processes used in industry have suggested new experimental appliances and operations in science; the wealth rolled up in business has to some extent been diverted to endowment of research. The uninterrupted and pervasive interaction of scientific discovery and industrial application has fructified both science and industry, and has brought home to the contemporary mind the fact that the gist of scientific knowledge is control of natural energies. These four facts, natural science, experimentation, control and progress have been inextricably bound up together. That up to the present the application of the newer methods and results has influenced the means of life rather than its ends; or, better put, that human aims have so far been affected in an accidental rather than in an intelligently directed way, signifies that so far the change has been technical rather than human and moral, that it has been economic rather than adequately social. Put in the language of Bacon, this means that while we have been reasonably successful in obtaining command of nature by means of science, our science is not yet such that this command is systematically and preeminently applied to the relief of human estate. Such applications occur and in great numbers, but they are incidental, sporadic and external. And this limitation defines the specific problem of philosophical reconstruction at the present time. For it emphasizes the larger social deficiencies that require intelligent diagnosis, and projection of aims and methods.

It is hardly necessary to remind you however that marked political changes have already followed upon the new science and its industrial applications, and that in so far some directions of social development have at least been marked out. The growth of the new technique of industry has everywhere been followed by the fall of feudal institutions, in which the social pattern was formed in agricultural occupations and military pursuits. Wherever business in the modern sense has gone, the tendency has been to transfer power from land to financial capital, from the country to the city, from the farm to factory, from social titles based on personal allegiance, service and protection, to those based on control of labor and exchange of goods. The change in the political centre of gravity has resulted in emancipating the individual from bonds of class and custom and in producing a political organization which depends less upon superior authority and more upon voluntary choice. Modern states, in other words, are regarded less as divine, and more as human works than they used to be; less as necessary manifestations of some supreme and over-ruling principles, and more as contrivances of men and women to realize their own desires.

The contract theory of the origin of the state is a theory whose falsity may easily be demonstrated both philosophically and historically. Nevertheless this theory has had great currency and influence. In form, it stated that some time in the past men voluntarily got together and made a compact with one another to observe certain laws and to submit to certain authority and in that way brought the state and the relation of ruler and subject into existence. Like many things in philosophy, the theory, though worthless as a record of fact, is of great worth as a symptom of the direction of human desire. It testified to a growing belief that the state existed to satisfy human needs and could be shaped by human intention and volition. Aristotle's theory that the state exists by nature failed to satisfy the thought of the seventeenth century because it seemed by making the state a product of nature to remove its constitution beyond human choice. Equally significant was the assumption of the contract theory that individuals by their personal decisions expressing their personal wishes bring the state into existence. The rapidity with which the theory gained a hold all over western Europe showed the extent to which the bonds of customary institutions had relaxed their grip. It proved that men had been so liberated from absorption in larger groups that they were conscious of themselves as individuals having rights and claims on their own account, not simply as members of a class, guild or social grade.

Side by side with this political individualism went a religious and moral individualism. The metaphysical doctrine of the superiority of the species to the individual, of the permanent universal to the changing particular, was the philosophic support of political and ecclesiastical institutionalism. The universal church was the ground, end and limit of the individual's beliefs and acts in spiritual matters, just as the feudal hierarchical organization was the basis, law and fixed limit of his behavior in secular affairs. The northern barbarians had never completely come under the sway of classic ideas and customs. That which was indigenous where life was primarily derived from Latin sources was borrowed and more or less externally imposed in Germanic Europe. Protestantism marked the formal breaking away from the domination of Roman ideas. It effected liberation of individual conscience and worship from control by an organized institution claiming to be permanent and universal. It cannot truly be said that at the outset the new religious movement went far in promoting freedom of thought and criticism, or in denying the notion of some supreme authority to which individual intelligence was absolutely in bonds. Nor at first did it go far in furthering tolerance or respect for divergency of moral and religious convictions. But practically it did tend to disintegration of established institutions. By multiplying sects and churches it encouraged at least a negative toleration of the right of individuals to judge ultimate matters for themselves. In time, there developed a formulated belief in the sacredness of individual conscience and in the right to freedom of opinion, belief and worship.

It is unnecessary to point out how the spread of this conviction increased political individualism, or how it accelerated the willingness of men to question received ideas in science and philosophy—to think and observe and experiment for themselves. Religious individualism served to supply a much needed sanction to initiative and independence of thought in all spheres, even when religious movements officially were opposed to such freedom when carried beyond a limited point. The greatest influence of Protestantism was, however, in developing

the idea of the personality of every human being as an
end in himself. When human beings were regarded as
capable of direct relationship with God, without the
intermediary of any organization like the Church, and
the drama of sin, redemption and salvation was something enacted within the innermost soul of individuals
rather than in the species of which the individual was a
subordinate part, a fatal blow was struck at all doctrines which taught the subordination of personality—
a blow which had many political reverberations in
promoting democracy. For when in religion the idea of
the intrinsic worth of every soul as such was proclaimed,
it was difficult to keep the idea from spilling over, so to
say, into secular relationships.

The absurdity is obvious of trying in a few paragraphs to summarize movements in industry, politics and
religion whose influence is still far from exhausted and
about which hundreds and thousands of volumes have
been written. But I shall count upon your forbearance
to recall that these matters are alluded to only in order
to suggest some of the forces that operated to mark out
the channels in which new ideas ran. First, there is the
transfer of interest from the eternal and universal to
what is changing and specific, concrete—a movement
that showed itself practically in carrying over of attention and thought from another world to this, from the
supernaturalism characteristic of the Middle Ages

to delight in natural science, natural activity and natural intercourse. Secondly, there is the gradual decay of the authority of fixed institutions and class distinctions and relations, and a growing belief in the power of individual minds, guided by methods of observation, experiment and reflection, to attain the truths needed for the guidance of life. The operations and results of natural inquiry gained in prestige and power at the expense of principles dictated from high authority.

Consequently principles and alleged truths are judged more and more by criteria of their origin in experience and their consequences of weal and woe in experience, and less by criteria of sublime origin from beyond everyday experience and independent of fruits in experience. It is no longer enough for a principle to be elevated, noble, universal and hallowed by time. It must present its birth certificate, it must show under just what conditions of human experience it was generated, and it must justify itself by its works, present and potential. Such is the inner meaning of the modern appeal to experience as an ultimate criterion of value and validity. In the third place, great store is set upon the idea of progress. The future rather than the past dominates the imagination. The Golden Age lies ahead of us not behind us. Everywhere new possibilities beckon and arouse courage and effort. The great

French thinkers of the later eighteenth century borrowed this idea from Bacon and developed it into the doctrine of the indefinite perfectibility of mankind on earth. Man is capable, if he will but exercise the required courage, intelligence and effort, of shaping his own fate. Physical conditions offer no insurmountable barriers. In the fourth place, the patient and experimental study of nature, bearing fruit in inventions which control nature and subdue her forces to social uses, is the method by which progress is made. Knowledge is power and knowledge is achieved by sending the mind to school to nature to learn her processes of change.

In this lecture as in the previous one, I can hardly close better than by reference to the new responsibilities imposed upon philosophy and the new opportunities opened to it. Upon the whole, the greatest effect of these changes up to date has been to substitute an Idealism based on epistemology, or the theory of knowledge, for the Idealism based on the metaphysics of classic antiquity.

Earlier modern philosophy (even though unconsciously to itself) had the problem of reconciling the traditional theory of the rational and ideal basis, stuff and end of the universe with the new interest in individual mind and the new confidence in its capacities. It was in a dilemma. On the one hand, it had no intention

of losing itself in a materialism which subordinated man
to physical existence and mind to matter—especially
just at the moment when in actual affairs man and mind
were beginning to achieve genuine rule over nature.
On the other hand, the conception that the world as
it stood was an embodiment of a fixed and comprehensive
Mind or Reason was uncongenial to those whose main
concern was with the deficiencies of the world and with
an attempt to remedy them. The effect of the objective
theological idealism that had developed out of classic
metaphysical idealism was to make the mind submissive
and acquiescent. The new individualism chafed under
the restrictions imposed upon it by the notion of a universal reason which had once and for all shaped nature
and destiny.

In breaking away from antique and medieval thought,
accordingly, early modern thought continued the older
tradition of a Reason that creates and constitutes the
world, but combined it with the notion that this Reason
operates through the human mind, individual or collective. This is the common note of idealism sounded by
all the philosophies of the seventeenth and eighteenth
centuries, whether belonging to the British school of
Locke, Berkeley and Hume or the Continental school of
Descartes. In Kant as everybody knows the two
strains came together; and the theme of the formation
of the knowable world by means of a thought that

operated exclusively through the human knower became explicit. Idealism ceased to be metaphysical and cosmic in order to become epistemological and personal.

It is evident that this development represents merely a transitional stage. It tried, after all, to put the new wine in the old bottles. It did not achieve a free and unbiased formulation of the meaning of the power to direct nature's forces through knowledge—that is, purposeful, experimental action acting to reshape beliefs and institutions. The ancient tradition was still strong enough to project itself unconsciously into men's ways of thinking, and to hamper and compromise the expression of the really modern forces and aims. Essential philosophic reconstruction represents an attempt to state these causes and results in a way freed from incompatible inherited factors. It will regard intelligence not as the original shaper and final cause of things, but as the purposeful energetic re-shaper of those phases of nature and life that obstruct social well-being. It esteems the individual not as an exaggeratedly self-sufficient Ego which by some magic creates the world, but as the agent who is responsible through initiative, inventiveness and intelligently directed labor for re-creating the world, transforming it into an instrument and possession of intelligence.

The train of ideas represented by the Baconian Knowledge is Power thus failed in getting an emancipated and independent expression. These become hopelessly entangled in standpoints and prepossessions that embodied a social, political and scientific tradition with which they were completely incompatible. The obscurity, the confusion of modern philosophy is the product of this attempt to combine two things which cannot possibly be combined either logically or morally. Philosophic reconstruction for the present is thus the endeavor to undo the entanglement and to permit the Baconian aspirations to come to a free and unhindered expression. In succeeding lectures we shall consider the needed reconstruction as it affects certain classic philosophic antitheses, like those of experience and reason, the real and the ideal. But first we shall have to consider the modifying effect exercised upon philosophy by that changed conception of nature, animate and inanimate, which we owe to the progress of science.

CHAPTER III

THE SCIENTIFIC FACTOR IN RECONSTRUC-
TION OF PHILOSOPHY

PHILOSOPHY starts from some deep and wide way of responding to the difficulties life presents, but it grows only when material is at hand for making this practical response conscious, articulate and communicable. Accompanying the economic, political and ecclesiastical changes which were alluded to in an earlier lecture, was a scientific revolution enormous in scope and leaving unchanged almost no detail of belief about nature, physical and human. In part this scientific transformation was produced by just the change in practical attitude and temper. But as it progressed, it furnished that change an appropriate vocabulary, congenial to its needs, and made it articulate. The advance of science in its larger generalizations and in its specific detail of fact supplied precisely that intellectual equipment of ideas and concrete fact that was needed in order to formulate, precipitate, communicate and propagate the new disposition. Today, accordingly, we shall deal with those contrasting conceptions of the structure and constitution of Nature, which when they are accepted on the

53

authority of science (alleged or real), form the intellectual framework of philosophy.

Contrasting conceptions of ancient and modern science have been selected. For I see no way in which the truly philosophic import of the picture of the world painted by modern science can be appreciated except to exhibit it in contrast with that earlier picture which gave classic metaphysics its intellectual foundation and confirmation. The world in which philosophers once put their trust was a closed world, a world consisting internally of a limited number of fixed forms, and having definite boundaries externally. The world of modern science is an open world, a world varying indefinitely without the possibility of assignable limit in its internal make-up, a world stretching beyond any assignable bounds externally. Again, the world in which even the most intelligent men of olden times thought they lived was a fixed world, a realm where changes went on only within immutable limits of rest and permanence, and a world where the fixed and unmoving was, as we have already noted. higher in quality and authority than the moving and altering. And in the third place, the world which men once saw with their eyes, portrayed in their imaginations and repeated in their plans of conduct, was a world of a limited number of classes, kinds, forms, distinct in quality (as kinds and species must be distinct) and arranged in a graded order of superiority and inferiority.

It is not easy to recall the image of the universe which was taken for granted in the world tradition. In spite of its dramatic rendering (as in Dante), of the dialectical elaborations of Aristotle and St. Thomas, in spite of the fact that it held men's minds captive until the last three hundred years, and that its overthrow involved a religious upheaval, it is already dim, faded and remote. Even as a separate and abstract thing of theory it is not easy to recover.

As something pervasive, interwoven with all the details of reflection and observation, with the plans and rules of behavior, it is impossible to call it back again. Yet, as best we can, we need to put before our minds a definitely enclosed universe, something which can be called a universe in a literal and visible sense, having the earth at its fixed and unchanging centre and at a fixed circumference the heavenly arch of fixed stars moving in an eternal round of divine ether, hemming in all things and keeping them forever at one and in order. The earth, though at the centre, is the coarsest, grossest, most material, least significant and good (or perfect) of the parts of this closed world. It is the scene of maximum fluctuation and vicissitude. It is the least rational, and therefore the least notable, or knowable; it offers the least to reward contemplation, provoke

admiration and govern conduct. Between this grossly
material centre and the immaterial, spiritual and eternal
heavens lie a definite series of regions of moon, planets,
sun, etc., each of which gains in rank, value, rationality
and true being as it is farther from earth and nearer
the heavens. Each of these regions is composed of its
own appropriate stuff of earth, water, air, fire in its
own dominant degree, until we reach the heavenly firma-
ment which transcends all these principles, being constituted, as was just said, of that immaterial, inalterable
energy called ether.

Within this tight and pent in universe, changes take
place of course. But they are only of a small number
of fixed kinds; and they operate only within fixed limits.
Each kind of stuff has its own appropriate motion. It
is the nature of earthly things to be heavy, since they
are gross, and hence to move downward. Fire and
superior things are light and hence move upward to
their proper place; air rises only to the plane of the
planets, where it then takes its back and forth motion
which naturally belongs to it, as is evident in the winds
and in respiration. Ether being the highest of all
physical things has a purely circular movement. The
daily return of the fixed stars is the closest possible
approximation to eternity, and to the self-involved revolution of mind upon its own ideal axis of reason. Upon
the earth in virtue of its earthly nature—or rather its

lack of virtue—is a scene of mere change. Mere flux, aimless and meaningless, starts at no definite point and arrives at nothing, amounts to nothing. Mere changes of quantity, all purely mechanical changes, are of this kind. They are like the shiftings of the sands by the sea. They may be sensed, but they cannot be " noted " or understood; they lack fixed limits which govern them. They are contemptible. They are casual, the sport of accident.

Only changes which lead to some defined or fixed outcome of form are of any account and can have any account—any *logos* or reason—made of them. The growth of plants and animals illustrates the highest kind of change which is possible in the sublunary or mundane sphere. They go from one definite fixed form to another. Oaks generate only oaks, oysters only oysters, man only man. The material factor of mechanical production enters in, but enters in as accident to prevent the full consummation of the type of the species, and to bring about the meaningless variations which diversify various oaks or oysters from one another; **or in** extreme cases to produce freaks, sports, monsters, three-handed or four-toed men. Aside from accidental and undesirable variations, each individual has a fixed career to pursue, a fixed path in which to travel. Terms which sound modern, words like potentiality and development abound in Aristotelian thought,

and have misled some into reading into his thought
modern meanings. But the significance of these words
in classic and medieval thought is rigidly determined by
their context. Development holds merely of the course
of changes which takes place within a particular member of the species. It is only a name for the prede-
termined movement from the acorn to the oak tree. It
takes place not in things generally but only in some
one of the numerically insignificant members of the oak
species. Development, evolution, never means, as in
modern science, origin of new forms, a mutation from
an old species, but only the monotonous traversing of a
previously plotted cycle of change. So potentiality
never means, as in modern life, the possibility of novelty,
of invention, of radical deviation, but only that
principle in virtue of which the acorn becomes the oak.
Technically, it is the capacity for movement between
opposites. Only the cold can become hot; only the dry
can become wet; only the babe can become a man; the
seed the full-grown wheat and so on. Potentiality instead of implying the emergence of anything novel means
merely the facility with which a particular thing repeats the recurrent processes of its kind, and thus
becomes a specific case of the eternal forms in and
through which all things are constituted.

In spite of the almost infinite numerical diversity of
individuals, there are only a limited number of species,

kinds or sorts. And the world is essentially a world which falls into sorts; it is pre-arranged into distinct classes. Moreover, just as we naturally arrange plants and animals into series, ranks and grades, from the lower to the highest, so with all things in the universe. The distinct classes to which things belong by their very nature form a hierarchical order. There are castes in nature. The universe is constituted on an aristocratic, one can truly say a feudal, plan. Species, classes do not mix or overlap—except in cases of accident, and to the result of chaos. Otherwise, everything belongs in advance to a certain class, and the class has its own fixed place in the hierarchy of Being. The universe is indeed a tidy spot whose purity is interfered with only by those irregular changes in individuals which are due to the presence of an obdurate matter that refuses to yield itself wholly to rule and form. Otherwise it is a universe with a fixed place for everything and where everything knows its place, its station and class, and keeps it. Hence what are known technically as final and formal causes are supreme, and efficient causes are relegated to an inferior place. The so-called final cause is just a name for the fact that there is some fixed form characteristic of a class or sort of things which governs the changes going on, so that they tend toward it as their end and goal, the fulfilment of their true nature. The supralunar region is the end

or final cause of the proper movements of air and fire;
the earth of the motions of crass, heavy things; the oak
of the acorn; the mature form in general of the germi-
nal.

The " efficient cause," that which produces and in-
stigates a movement is only some external change as
it accidentally gives a kind of push to an immature,
imperfect being and starts it moving toward its perfected or fulfilled form. The final cause is the perfected form regarded as the *explanation or reason* of
prior changes. When it is not taken in reference to the
changes completed and brought to rest in it, but in
itself it is the " formal cause ": The inherent *nature*
or character which " makes " or constitutes a thing
what it is so far as it truly *is*, namely, what it is so far
as it does not change. Logically and practically all of
the traits which have been enumerated cohere. Attack
one and you attack all. When any one is undermined,
all go. This is the reason why the intellectual modification of the last few centuries may truly be called a
revolution. It has substituted a conception of the world
differing at every point. It makes little matter at what
point you commence to trace the difference, you find
yourself carried into all other points.

Instead of a closed universe, science now presents us
with one infinite in space and time, having no limits here
or there, at this end, so to speak, or at that, and as

infinitely complex in internal structure as it is infinite
in extent. Hence it is also an open world, an infinitely
variegated one, a world which in the old sense can
hardly be called a universe at all; so multiplex and
far-reaching that it cannot be summed up and grasped
in any one formula. And change rather than fixity is
now a measure of " reality " or energy of being; change
is omnipresent. The laws in which the modern man
of science is interested are laws of motion, of generation
and consequence. He speaks of law where the ancients
spoke of kind and essence, because what he wants is a
correlation of changes, an ability to detect one change
occurring in correspondence with another. He does not
try to define and delimit something remaining constant
in change. He tries to describe a constant order *of*
change. And while the word "constant" appears in
both statements, the meaning of the word is not the
same. In one case, we are dealing with something constant in *existence*, physical or metaphysical; in the
other case, with something constant in *function* and
operation. One is a form of independent being; the
other is a formula of description and calculation of
interdependent changes.

In short, classic thought accepted a feudally
arranged order of classes or kinds, each " holding "
from a superior and in turn giving the rule of conduct
and service to.an inferior. This trait reflects and

parallels most closely the social situation we were considering at the last hour. We have a fairly definite
notion of society as organized upon the feudal basis.
The family principle, the principle of kinship is strong,
and especially is this true as we ascend in the social
scale. At the lower end, individuals may be lost more or
less in the mass. Since all are parts of the common
herd, there is nothing especial to distinguish their birth.
But among the privileged and ruling class the case is
quite different. The tie of kinship at once marks a group
off externally and gives it distinction, and internally
holds all its members together. Kinship, kind, class,
genus are synonymous terms, starting from social and
concrete facts and going to the technical and abstract.
For kinship is a sign of a common nature, of something
universal and permanent running through all particular
individuals, and giving them a real and objective unity.
Because such and such persons are kin they are *really*,
and not merely conventionally, marked off into a class
having something unique about it. All contemporary
members are bound into an objective unity which includes ancestors and descendants and excludes all who
belong to another kin or kind. Assuredly this parcel-
ling out of the world into separate kinds, each having
its qualitatively distinct nature in contrast with other
species, binding numerically distinct individuals together, and preventing their diversities from exceeding

fixed bounds, may without exaggeration be called a projection of the family principle into the world at large.

In a feudally organized society, moreover, each kinship group or species occupies a definite place. It is marked by the possession of a specific *rank* higher or lower with respect to other grades. This position confers upon it certain privileges, enabling it to enforce certain claims upon those lower in the scale and entailing upon it certain services and homage to be rendered to superiors. The relationship of causation, so to speak, is up and down. Influence, power, proceeds from above to below; the activities of the inferior are performed with respect, quite literally, to what is above. Action and reaction are far from being equal and in opposite directions. All action is of one sort, of the nature of lordship, and proceeds from the higher to the lower. Reaction is of the nature of subjection and deference and proceeds from lower to higher. The classic theory of the constitution of the world corresponds point by point to this ordering of classes in a scale of dignity and power.

A third trait assigned by historians to feudalism is that the ordering of ranks centres about armed service and the relationship of armed defense and protection. I am afraid that what has already been said about the parallelism of ancient cosmology with social organization may seem a fanciful analogy; and if a comparison is also drawn in this last regard, there will be no doubt in your minds that a metaphor is being forced. Such is truly the case if we take the comparison too literally. But not so, if we confine our attention to the notion of rule and command implied in both. Attention has already been called to the meaning that is now given the term law—a constant relationship among changes. Nevertheless, we often hear about laws which " govern " events, and it often seems to be thought that phenomena would be utterly disorderly were there not laws to keep them in order. This way of thinking is a survival of reading social relationships into nature—not necessarily a feudal relationship, but the relation of ruler and ruled, sovereign and subject. Law is assimilated to a command or order. If the factor of personal will is eliminated (as it was in the best Greek thought) still the idea of law or universal is impregnated with the sense of a guiding and ruling influence exerted from above on what is naturally inferior to it. The universal governs as the end and model which the artisan has in mind " governs " his movements. The Middle Ages added to this Greek idea of control the idea of a command proceeding from a superior will; and hence thought of the operations of nature as if they were a fulfilment of a task set by one who had authority to direct action.

The traits of the picture of nature drawn by modern

science fairly spring by contrast into high relief. Modern science took its first step when daring astronomers abolished the distinction of high, sublime and ideal forces operating in the heavens from lower and material forces actuating terrestrial events. The supposed heterogeneity of substances and forces between heaven and earth was denied. It was asserted that the same laws hold everywhere, that there is homogeneity of material and process everywhere throughout nature. The remote and esthetically sublime is to be scientifically described and explained in terms of homely familiar events and forces. The material of direct handling and observation is that of which we are surest; it is the better known. Until we can convert the grosser and more superficial observations of far-away things in the heavens into elements identical with those of things directly at hand, they remain blind and not understood. Instead of presenting superior worth, they present only problems. They are not means of enlightenment but challenges. The earth is not superior in rank to sun, moon and stars, but it is equal in dignity, and its occurrences give the key to the understanding of celestial existences. Being *at* hand, they are also capable of being brought *under* our hand; they can be manipulated, broken up, resolved into elements which can be managed, combined at will in old and new forms. The net result may be termed, I think, without any great forcing, the substitution of a democracy of individual facts equal in rank for the feudal system of an ordered gradation of general classes of unequal rank.

One important incident of the new science was the destruction of the idea that the earth is the centre of the universe. When the idea of a fixed centre went, there went with it the idea of a closed universe and a circumscribing heavenly boundary. To the Greek sense, just because its theory of knowing was dominated by esthetic considerations, the finite was the perfect. Literally, the finite was the finished, the ended, the completed, that with no ragged edges and unaccountable operations. The infinite or limitless was lacking in character just because it was in-finite. Being everything, it was nothing. It was unformed and chaotic, uncontrolled and unruly, the source of incalculable deviations and accidents. Our present feeling that associates infinity with boundless power, with capacity for expansion that knows no end, with the delight in a progress that has no external limit, would be incomprehensible were it not that interest has shifted from the esthetic to the practical; from interest in beholding a harmonious and complete scene to interest in transforming an inharmonious one. One has only to read the authors of the transition period, say Giordano Bruno, to realize what a pent-in, suffocating sensation they associated with a closed, finite world, and what a

feeling of exhilaration, expansion and boundless possibility was aroused in them by the thought of a world
infinite in stretch of space and time, and composed
internally of infinitesimal infinitely numerous elements.
That which the Greeks withdrew from with repulsion
they welcomed with an intoxicated sense of adventure.
The infinite meant, it was true, something forever un-
traversed even by thought, and hence something forever
unknown—no matter how great attainment in learning.   But this " forever unknown " instead of being
chilling and repelling was now an inspiring challenge
to ever-renewed inquiry, and an assurance of inexhaustible possibilities of progress.

The student of history knows well that the Greeks
made great progress in the science of mechanics as well
as of geometry.   At first sight, it appears strange that
with this advance in mechanics so little advance was
made in the direction of modern science.   The seeming
paradox impels us to ask why it was that mechanics
remained a separate science, why it was not used in
description and explanation of natural phenomena after
the manner of Galileo and Newton.   The answer is
found in the social parallelism already mentioned.
Socially speaking, machines, tools, were devices employed by artisans.   The science of mechanics had to
do with the kind of things employed by human mechanics, and mechanics were base fellows.   They were at the

lower end of the social scale, and how could light on the
heavens, the highest, be derived from them? The application of considerations of mechanics to natural
phenomena would moreover have implied an interest in
the practical control and utilization of phenomena
which was totally incompatible with the importance
attached to final causes as fixed determiners of nature.
All the scientific reformers of the sixteenth and seventeenth centuries strikingly agree in regarding the doctrine of final causes as *the* cause of the failure of science.
Why? Because this doctrine taught that the processes
of nature are held in bondage to certain fixed ends which
they must tend to realize. Nature was kept in leading strings; it was cramped down to production of a
limited number of stereotyped results. Only a comparatively small number of things could be brought
into being, and these few must be similar to the ends
which similar cycles of change had effected in the past.
The scope of inquiry and understanding was limited to
the narrow round of processes eventuating in the fixed
ends which the observed world offered to view. At
best, invention and production of new results by use of
machines and tools must be restricted to articles of
transient dignity and bodily, not intellectual, use.

When the rigid clamp of fixed ends was taken off
from nature, observation and imagination were emancipated, and experimental control for scientific and prac-

tical purposes enormously stimulated. Because natural processes were no longer restricted to a fixed number of immovable ends or results, anything might conceivably happen. It was only a question of what elements could be brought into juxtaposition so that they would work upon one another. Immediately, mechanics ceased to be a separate science and became an organ for attacking nature. The mechanics of the lever, wheel, pulley and inclined plane told accurately what happens when things in space are used to move one another during definite periods of time. The whole of nature became a scene of pushes and pulls, of cogs and levers, of motions of parts or elements to which the formulae of movements produced by well-known machines were directly applicable.

The banishing of ends and forms from the universe has seemed to many an ideal and spiritual impoverishment. When nature was regarded as a set of mechanical interactions, it apparently lost all meaning and purpose. Its glory departed. Elimination of differences of quality deprived it of beauty. Denial to nature of all inherent longings and aspiring tendencies toward ideal ends removed nature and natural science from contact with poetry, religion and divine things. There seemed to be left only a harsh, brutal despiritualized exhibition of mechanical forces. As a consequence, it has seemed to many philosophers that one of their

chief problems was to reconcile the existence of this
purely mechanical world with belief in objective rationality and purpose—to save life from a degrading materialism.   Hence many sought to re-attain by way of
an analysis of the process of knowing, or epistemology,
that belief in the superiority of Ideal Being which had
anciently been maintained on the basis of cosmology.
But when it is recognized that the mechanical view is
determined by the requirements of an experimental control of natural energies, this problem of reconciliation
no longer vexes us.   Fixed forms and ends, let us recall,
mark fixed limits to change.   Hence they make futile all
human efforts to produce and regulate change except
within narrow and unimportant limits.   They paralyze
constructive human inventions by a theory which condemns them in advance to failure.   Human activity
can conform only to ends already set by nature.   It
was not till ends were banished from nature that purposes became important as factors in human minds
capable of reshaping existence.   A natural world that
does not subsist for the sake of realizing a fixed set of
ends is relatively malleable and plastic; it may be used
for this end *or* that.   That nature can be known through
the application of mechanical formulae is the prime
condition of turning it to human account.   Tools,
machines are means to be utilized.   Only when nature is
regarded as mechanical, is systematic invention and

construction of machines relevant to nature's activities. Nature is subdued to human purpose because it is no longer the slave of metaphysical and theological purpose.

Bergson has pointed out that man might well be called *Home Faber*. He is distinguished as the tool-making animal. This has held good since man was man; but till nature was construed in mechanical terms, the making of tools with which to attack and transform nature was sporadic and accidental. Under such circumstances it would not have occurred even to a Bergson that man's tool-making capacity was so important and fundamental that it could be used to define him. The very things that make the nature of the mechanical-physical scientist esthetically blank and dull are the things which render nature amenable to human control. When qualities were subordinated to quantitative and mathematical relationships, color, music and form disappeared from the object of the scientist's inquiry as such. But the remaining properties of weight, extension, numerable velocity of movement and so on were just the qualities which lent themselves to the substitution of one thing for another, to the conversion of one form of energy into another; to the effecting of transformations. When chemical fertilizers can be used in place of animal manures, when improved grain and cattle can be purposefully bred from inferior animals and grasses, when mechanical energy can be converted into heat and electricity into mechanical energy, man gains power to manipulate nature. Most of all he gains power to frame *new* ends and aims and to proceed in regular system to their actualization. Only indefinite substitution and convertibility regardless of quality render nature manageable. The mechanization of nature is the condition of a practical and progressive idealism in action.

It thus turns out that the old, old dread and dislike of matter as something opposed to mind and threatening it, to be kept within the narrowest bounds of recognition; something to be denied so far as possible lest it encroach upon ideal purposes and finally exclude them from the real world, is as absurd practically as it was impotent intellectually. Judged from the only scientific standpoint, what it does and how it functions, matter means conditions. To respect matter means to respect the conditions of achievement; conditions which hinder and obstruct and which have to be changed, conditions which help and further and which can be used to modify obstructions and attain ends. Only as men have learned to pay sincere and persistent regard to matter, to the conditions upon which depends negatively and positively the success of all endeavor, have they shown sincere and fruitful respect for ends and purposes. To profess to have an aim and then neglect

the means of its execution is self-delusion of the most
dangerous sort. Education and morals will begin to
find themselves on the same road of advance that say
chemical industry and medicine have found for themselves when they too learn fully the lesson of whole-
hearted and unremitting attention to means and conditions—that is, to what mankind so long despised as
material and mechanical. When we take means for ends
we indeed fall into moral materialism. But when we
take ends without regard to means we degenerate into
sentimentalism. In the name of the ideal we fall back
upon mere luck and chance and magic or exhortation
and preaching; or else upon a fanaticism that will
force the realization of preconceived ends at any
cost.

I have touched in this lecture upon many things in
a cursory way. Yet there has been but one point in
mind. The revolution in our conceptions of nature and
in our methods of knowing it has bred a new temper of
imagination and aspiration. It has confirmed the new
attitude generated by economic and political changes.
It has supplied this attitude with definite intellectual
material with which to formulate and justify itself.

In the first lecture it was noted that in Greek life
prosaic matter of fact or empirical knowledge was at
a great disadvantage as compared with the imaginative
beliefs that were bound up with special institutions

and moral habitudes. Now this empirical knowledge has grown till it has broken its low and limited sphere of application and esteem. It has itself become an organ of inspiring imagination through introducing ideas of boundless possibility, indefinite progress, free movement, equal opportunity irrespective of fixed limits. It has reshaped social institutions, and in so far developed a new morale. It has achieved ideal values. It is convertible into creative and constructive philosophy.

Convertible, however, rather than already converted. When we consider how deeply embedded in customs of thought and action the classic philosophy came to be and how congenial it is to man's more spontaneous beliefs, the throes that attended its birth are not to be wondered at. We should rather wonder that a view so upsetting, so undermining, made its way without more persecutions, martyrdoms and disturbances. It certainly is not surprising that its complete and consistent formulation in philosophy has been long delayed. The main efforts of thinkers were inevitably directed to minimizing the shock of change, easing the strains of transition, mediating and reconciling. When we look back upon almost all of the thinkers of the seventeenth and eighteenth centuries, upon all excepting those who were avowedly sceptical and revolutionary, what strikes us is the amount of traditional subject-matter and method that is to be found even among those who were regarded as most advanced. Men cannot easily throw off their old habits of thinking, and never can throw off all of them at once. In developing, teaching and receiving new ideas we are compelled to use some of the old ones as tools of understanding and communication. Only piecemeal, step-by-step, could the full import of the new science be grasped. Roughly speaking, the seventeenth century witnessed its application in astronomy and general cosmology; the eighteenth century in physics and chemistry; the nineteenth century undertook an application in geology and the biological sciences.

It was said that it has now become extremely difficult to recover the view of the world which universally obtained in Europe till the seventeenth century. Yet after all we need only recur to the science of plants and animals as it was before Darwin and to the ideas which even now are dominant in moral and political matters to find the older order of conceptions in full possession of the popular mind. Until the dogma of fixed unchangeable types and species, of arrangement in classes of higher and lower, of subordination of the transitory individual to the universal or kind had been shaken in its hold upon the science of life, it was impossible that the new ideas and method should be made at home in social and moral life. Does it not seem to be the intellectual task of the twentieth century to take this last step? When this step is taken the circle of scientific development will be rounded out and the reconstruction of philosophy be made an accomplished fact.

CHAPTER IV

CHANGED CONCEPTIONS OF EXPERIENCE AND REASON

WHAT is experience and what is Reason, Mind? What is the scope of experience and what are its limits? How far is it a sure ground of belief and a safe guide of conduct? Can we trust it in science and in behavior? Or is it a quagmire as soon as we pass beyond a few low material interests? Is it so shaky, shifting, and shallow that instead of affording sure footing, safe paths to fertile fields, it misleads, betrays, and engulfs? Is a Reason outside experience and above it needed to supply assured principles to science and conduct? In one sense, these questions suggest technical problems of abstruse philosophy; in another sense, they contain the deepest possible questionings regarding the career of man. They concern the criteria he is to employ in forming his beliefs; the principles *by* which he is to direct his life and the ends *to* which he is to direct it. Must man transcend experience by some organ of unique character that carries him into the super-empirical? Failing this, must he wander sceptical and disillusioned? Or is human experience itself worth while in its purposes and its methods of guidance? Can it organize itself into stable courses or must it be sustained from without?

We know the answers of traditional philosophy. They do not thoroughly agree among themselves, but they agree that experience never rises above the level of the particular, the contingent, and the probable. Only a power transcending in origin and content any and all conceivable experience can attain to universal, necessary and certain authority and direction. The empiricists themselves admitted the correctness of these assertions. They only said that since there is no faculty of Pure Reason in the possession of mankind, we must put up with what we have, experience, and make the most possible out of it. They contented themselves with sceptical attacks upon the transcendentalist, with indications of the ways in which we might best seize the meaning and good of the passing moment; or like Locke, asserted that in spite of the limitation of experience, it affords the light needed to guide men's footsteps modestly in conduct. They affirmed that the alleged authoritative guidance by a higher faculty had practically hampered men.

It is the function of this lecture to show how and why it is now possible to make claims for experience as a guide in science and moral life which the older empiricists did not and could not make for it.

Curiously enough, the key to the matter may be found in the fact that the old notion of experience was itself a product of experience—the only kind of experience which was then open to men. If another conception of experience is now possible, it is precisely because the quality of experience as it may now be lived has undergone a profound social and intellectual change from that of earlier times. The account of experience which we find in Plato and Aristotle is an account of what Greek experience actually was. It agrees very closely with what the modern psychologist knows as the method of learning by trial and error as distinct from the method of learning by ideas. Men tried certain acts, they underwent certain sufferings and affections. Each of these in the time of its occurrence is isolated, particular—its counterpart is transient appetite and transient sensation. But memory preserves and accumulates these separate incidents. As they pile up, irregular variations get cancelled, common features are selected, reinforced and combined. Gradually a habit of action is built up, and corresponding to this habit there forms a certain generalized picture of an object or situation. We come to know or note not merely this particular which as a particular cannot strictly be known at all (for not being classed it cannot be characterized and identified) but to recognize it as man, tree, stone, leather —an individual of a certain kind, marked by a certain

universal form characteristic of a whole species of thing.
Along with the development of this common-sense
knowledge, there grows up a certain regularity of conduct. The particular incidents fuse, and a *way* of acting which is general, as far as it goes, builds up. The
skill develops which is shown by the artisan, the shoemaker, the carpenter, the gymnast, the physician, who
have regular ways of handling cases. This regularity
signifies, of course, that the particular case is not
treated as an isolated particular, but as one of a kind,
which therefore demands a *kind* of action. From the
multitude of particular illnesses encountered, the physician in learning to class some of them as indigestion
learns also to treat the cases of the class in a common
or general way. He forms the rule of recommending a
certain diet, and prescribing a certain remedy. All this
forms what we call experience. It results, as the illustration shows, in a certain general insight and a certain
organized ability in action.

But needless to insist, the generality and the organization are restricted and fallible. They hold, as Aristotle was fond of pointing out, usually, in most cases,
as a rule, but not universally, of necessity, or as a
principle. The physician is bound to make mistakes,
because individual cases are bound to vary unaccount-
ably: such is their very nature. The difficulty does not
arise in *a* defective experience which is capable of

remedy in some better experience. Experience itself, as such, is defective, and hence default is inevitable and irremediable. The only universality and certainty is in a region above experience, that of the rational and conceptual. As the particular was a stepping-stone to image and habit, so the latter may become a stepping-stone to conceptions and principles. But the latter leave experience behind, untouched; they do not react to rectify it. Such is the notion which still lingers in the contrast of " empirical " and " rational " as when we say that a certain architect or physician is empirical, not scientific in his procedures. But the difference between the classic and the modern notion of experience is revealed in the fact that such a statement is now a charge, a disparaging accusation, brought against *a* particular architect or physician. With Plato, Aristotle and the Scholastic, it was a charge against the callings, since they were modes of experience. It was an indictment of all practical action in contrast with conceptual contemplation.

The modern philosopher who has professed himself an empiricist has usually had a critical purpose in mind. Like Bacon, Locke, Condillac and Helvetius, he stood face to face with a body of beliefs and a set of institutions in which he profoundly disbelieved. His problem was the problem of attack upon so much dead weight carried uselessly by humanity, crushing and distorting it. His readiest way of undermining and disintegrating was by appealing to experience as a final test and criterion. In every case, active reformers were " empiricists " in the philosophical sense. They made it their business to show that some current belief or institution that claimed the sanction of innate ideas or necessary conceptions, or an origin in an authoritative revelation of reason, had in fact proceeded from a lowly origin in experience, and had been confirmed by accident, by class interest or by biased authority.

The philosophic empiricism initiated by Locke was thus disintegrative in intent. It optimistically took it for granted that when the burden of blind custom, imposed authority, and accidental associations was removed, progress in science and social organization would spontaneously take place. Its part was to help in removing the burden. The best way to liberate men from the burden was through a natural history of the origin and growth in the mind of the ideas connected with objectionable beliefs and customs. Santayana justly calls the psychology of this school a malicious psychology. It tended to identify the history of the formation of certain ideas with an account of the things to which the ideas refer—an identification which naturally had an unfavorable effect on the things. But Mr. Santayana neglects to notice the social zeal and aim latent in the malice. He fails to point out that this "malice" was aimed at institutions and traditions which had lost their usefulness; he fails to point out that to a large extent it was true of them that an account of their psychological origin was equivalent to a destructive account of the things themselves. But after Hume with debonair clarity pointed out that the analysis of beliefs into sensations and associations left "natural" ideas and institutions in the same position in which the reformers had placed "artificial" ones, the situation changed. The rationalists employed the logic of sensationalistic-empiricism to show that experience, giving only a heap of chaotic and isolated particulars, is as fatal to science and to moral laws and obligations as to obnoxious institutions; and concluded that "Reason" must be resorted to if experience was to be furnished with any binding and connecting principles. The new rationalistic idealism of Kant and his successors seemed to be necessitated by the totally destructive results of the new empirical philosophy.

Two things have rendered possible a new conception of experience and a new conception of the relation of reason to experience, or, more accurately, of the place of reason *in* experience. The primary factor is the change that has taken place in the actual nature of experience, its contents and methods, as it is actually lived. The other is the development of a psychology based upon biology which makes possible a new scientific formulation of the nature of experience.

Let us begin with the technical side—the change in psychology. We are only just now commencing to appreciate how completely exploded is the psychology that dominated philosophy throughout the eighteenth and nineteenth centuries. According to this theory, mental life originated in sensations which are separately and passively received, and which are formed, through laws of retention and association, into a mosaic of images, perceptions, and conceptions. The senses were regarded as gateways or avenues of knowledge. Except in combining atomic sensations, the mind was wholly passive and acquiescent in knowing. Volition, action, emotion, and desire follow in the wake of sensations and images. The intellectual or cognitive factor comes first and emotional and volitional life is only a consequent conjunction of ideas with sensations of pleasure and pain.

The effect of the development of biology has been to reverse the picture. Wherever there is life, there is behavior, activity. In order that life may persist, this activity has to be both continuous and adapted to the environment. This adaptive adjustment, moreover, is not wholly passive; is not a mere matter of the moulding of the organism by the environment. Even a clam acts upon the environment and modifies it to some extent. It selects materials for food and for the shell that

protects it.   It does something to the environment as
well as has something done to itself.   There is no such
thing in a living creature as mere conformity to conditions, though parasitic forms may approach this limit.
In the interests of the maintenance of life there is transformation of some elements in the surrounding medium.
The higher the form of life, the more important is the
active reconstruction of the medium.   This increased
control may be illustrated by the contrast of savage
with civilized man.   Suppose the two are living in a
wilderness.   With the savage there is the maximum of
accommodation to given conditions; the minimum of
what we may call hitting back.   The savage takes things
" as they are," and by using caves and roots and occasional pools leads a meagre and precarious existence.
The civilized man goes to distant mountains and dams
streams.   He builds reservoirs, digs channels, and con-
ducts the waters to what had been a desert.   He
searches the world to find plants and animals that will
thrive.   He takes native plants and by selection and
cross-fertilization improves them.   He introduces machinery to till the soil and care for the harvest.   By
such means he may succeed in making the wilderness
blossom like the rose.

Such transformation scenes are so familiar that we
overlook their meaning.   We forget that the inherent
power of life is illustrated in them.   Note what a change

this point of view entails in the traditional notions of experience. Experience becomes an affair primarily of doing. The organism does not stand about, Micawber-like, waiting for something to turn up. It does not wait passive and inert for something to impress itself upon it from without. The organism acts in accordance with its own structure, simple or complex, upon its surroundings. As a consequence the changes produced in the environment react upon the organism and its activities. The living creature undergoes, suffers, the consequences of its own behavior. This close connection between doing and suffering or undergoing forms what we call experience. Disconnected doing and disconnected suffering are neither of them experiences. Suppose fire encroaches upon a man when he is asleep. Part of his body is burned away. The burn does not perceptibly result from what he has done. There is nothing which in any instructive way can be named experience. Or again there is a series of mere activities, like twitchings of muscles in a spasm. The movements amount to nothing; they have no consequences for life. Or, if they have, these consequences are not connected with prior doing. There is no experience, no learning, no cumulative process. But suppose a busy infant puts his finger in the fire; the doing is random, aimless, without intention or reflection. But something happens in consequence. The child undergoes heat, he suffers pain.

The doing and undergoing, the reaching and the burn, are connected. One comes to suggest and mean the other. Then there is experience in a vital and significant sense.

Certain important implications for philosophy follow. In the first place, the interaction of organism and environment, resulting in some adaptation which secures utilization of the latter, is the primary fact, the basic category. Knowledge is relegated to a derived position, secondary in origin, even if its importance, when once it is established, is overshadowing. Knowledge is not something separate and self-sufficing, but is involved in the process by which life is sustained and evolved. The senses lose their place as gateways of knowing to take their rightful place as stimuli to action. To an animal an affection of the eye or ear is not an idle piece of information about something indifferently going on in the world. It is an invitation and inducement to act in a needed way. It is a clue in behavior, a directive factor in adaptation of life in its surroundings. It is urgent not cognitive in quality. The whole controversy between empiricism and rationalism as to the intellectual worth of sensations is rendered strangely obsolete. The discussion of sensations belongs under the head of immediate stimulus and response, not under the head of knowledge.

As a *conscious* element, a sensation marks an interruption in a course of action previously entered upon. Many psychologists since the time of Hobbes have dwelt upon what they call the relativity of sensations. We *feel* or sense cold in transition from warmth rather than absolutely; hardness is sensed upon a background of less resistance; a color in contrast with pure light or pure dark or in contrast with some other hue. A continuously unchanged tone or color cannot be attended to or sensed. What we take to be such monotonously prolonged sensations are in truth constantly interrupted by incursions of other elements, and represent a series of excursions back and forth. This fact was, however, misconstrued into a doctrine about the nature of knowledge. Rationalists used it to discredit sense as a valid or high mode of knowing things, since according to it we never get hold of anything *in itself* or intrinsically. Sensationalists used it to disparage all pretence at absolute knowledge.

Properly speaking, however, this fact of the relativity of sensation does not in the least belong in the sphere of knowing. Sensations of this sort are emotional and practical rather than cognitive and intellectual. They are shocks of change, due to interruption of a prior adjustment. They are signals to redirections of action. Let me take a trivial illustration. The person who is taking notes has no sensation of the pressure of his pencil on the paper or on his hand as long

as it functions properly. It operates merely as stimulus
to ready and effective adjustment. The sensory activity
incites automatically and unconsciously its proper
motor response. There is a preformed physiological
connection, acquired from habit but ultimately going
back to an original connection in the nervous system.
If the pencil-point gets broken or too blunt and the
habit of writing does not operate smoothly, there is a
conscious shock:—the feeling of something the matter,
something gone wrong. This emotional change operates
as a stimulus to a needed change in operation. One
looks at his pencil, sharpens it or takes another pencil
from one's pocket. The sensation operates as a pivot
of readjusting behavior. It marks a break in the
prior routine of writing and the beginning of some other
mode of action. Sensations are " relative " in the sense
of marking transitions in habits of behavior from one
course to another way of behaving.

The rationalist was thus right in denying that sensations as such are true elements of knowledge. But the
reasons he gave for this conclusion and the consequences
he drew from it were all wrong. Sensations are not
parts of *any* knowledge, good or bad, superior or inferior, imperfect or complete. They are rather provo-
cations, incitements, challenges to an act of inquiry
which is to *terminate* in knowledge. They are not ways
of knowing things inferior in value to reflective ways, to

the ways that require thought and inference, because they are not ways of knowing at all. They are stimuli to reflection and inference. As interruptions, they raise the questions: What does this shock mean? What is happening? What is the matter? How is my relation to the environment disturbed? What should be done about it? How shall I alter my course of action to meet the change that has taken place in the surroundings? How shall I readjust my behavior in response? Sensation is thus, as the sensationalist claimed, the beginning of knowledge, but only in the sense that the experienced shock of change is the necessary stimulus to the investigating and comparing which eventually produce knowledge.

When experience is aligned with the life-process and sensations are seen to be points of readjustment, the alleged atomism of sensations totally disappears. With this disappearance is abolished the need for a synthetic faculty of super-empirical reason to connect them. Philosophy is not any longer confronted with the hopeless problem of finding a way in which separate grains of sand may be woven into a strong and coherent rope —or into the illusion and pretence of one. When the isolated and simple existences of Locke and Hume are seen not to be truly empirical at all but to answer to certain demands of their theory of mind, the necessity ceases for the elaborate Kantian and Post-Kantian machinery of *a priori* concepts and categories to synthesize the alleged stuff of experience. The true " stuff " of experience is recognized to be adaptive courses of action, habits, active functions, connections of doing and undergoing; sensori-motor co-ordinations. Experience carries principles of connection and organization within itself. These principles are none the worse because they are vital and practical rather than epistemological. Some degree of organization is indispensable to even the lowest grade of life. Even an amoeba must have some continuity in time in its activity and some adaptation to its environment in space. Its life and experience cannot possibly consist in momentary, atomic, and self-enclosed sensations. Its activity has reference to its surroundings and to what goes before and what comes after. This organization intrinsic to life renders unnecessary a super-natural and super-empirical synthesis. It affords the basis and material for a positive evolution of intelligence as an organizing factor within experience.

Nor is it entirely aside from the subject to point out the extent in which social as well as biological organization enters into the formation of human experience. Probably one thing that strengthened the idea that the mind is passive and receptive in knowing was the observation of the helplessness of the human infant. But the observation points in quite another direction.

Because of his physical dependence and impotency, the contacts of the little child with nature are mediated by other persons. Mother and nurse, father and older children, determine what experiences the child shall have; they constantly instruct him as to the meaning of what he does and undergoes. The conceptions that are socially current and important become the child's principles of interpretation and estimation long before he attains to personal and deliberate control of conduct. Things come to him clothed in language, not in physical nakedness, and this garb of communication makes him a sharer in the beliefs of those about him. These beliefs coming to him as so many facts form his mind; they furnish the centres about which his own personal expeditions and perceptions are ordered. Here we have " categories " of connection and unification as important as those of Kant, but empirical not mythological.

From these elementary, if somewhat technical considerations, we turn to the change which experience itself has undergone in the passage from ancient and medieval to modern life. To Plato, experience meant enslavement to the past, to custom. Experience was almost equivalent to established customs formed not by reason or under intelligent control but by repetition and blind rule of thumb. Only reason can lift us above subjection to the accidents of the past. When we come to Bacon and his successors, we discover a curious re-

versal. Reason and its bodyguard of general notions
is now the conservative, mind-enslaving factor. Experience is the liberating power. Experience means the
new, that which calls us away from adherence to the
past, that which reveals novel facts and truths. Faith
in experience produces not devotion to custom but endeavor for progress. This difference in temper is the
more significant because it was so unconsciously taken
for granted. Some concrete and vital change must have
occurred in actual experience as that is lived. For,
after all, the thought of experience follows after and
is modelled upon the experience actually undergone.

When mathematics and other rational sciences developed among the Greeks, scientific truths did not
react back into daily experience. They remained
isolated, apart and super-imposed. Medicine was the
art in which perhaps the greatest amount of positive knowledge was obtained, but it did not reach
the dignity of science. It remained an art. In
practical arts, moreover, there was no conscious invention or purposeful improvement. Workers followed patterns that were handed down to them, while
departure from established standards and models
usually resulted in degenerate productions. Improvements came either from a slow, gradual, and un-
acknowledged accumulation of changes or else from
some sudden inspiration, which at once set a new stand-

ard. Being the result of no conscious method, it was fittingly attributed to the gods. In the social arts, such a radical reformer as Plato felt that existing evils were due to the absence of such fixed patterns as controlled the productions of artisans. The ethical purport of philosophy was to furnish them, and when once they were instituted, they were to be consecrated by religion, adorned by art, inculcated by education and enforced by magistrates so that alteration of them would be impossible.

It is unnecessary to repeat what has been so often dwelt upon as to the effect of experimental science in enabling man to effect a deliberate control of his environment. But since the impact of this control upon the traditional notion of experience is often overlooked, we must point out that when experience ceased to be empirical and became experimental, something of radical importance occurred. Aforetime man employed the results of his prior experience only to form customs that henceforth had to be blindly followed or blindly broken. Now, old experience is used to suggest aims and methods for developing a new and improved experience. Consequently experience becomes in so far constructively self-regulative. What Shakespeare so pregnantly said of nature, it is " made better by no mean, but nature makes that mean," becomes true of experience. We do not merely have to repeat the past, or wait for accidents to force change upon us. We *use* our past experiences to construct new and better ones in the future. The very fact of experience thus includes the process by which it directs itself in its own betterment.

Science, " reason " is not therefore something laid from above upon experience. Suggested and tested in experience, it is also employed through inventions in a thousand ways to expand and enrich experience. Although, as has been so often repeated, this self-creation and self-regulation of experience is still largely technological rather than truly artistic or human, yet what has been achieved contains the guaranty of the possibility of an intelligent administering of experience. The limits are moral and intellectual, due to defects in our good will and knowledge. They are not inherent metaphysically in the very nature of experience. " Reason " as a faculty separate from experience, introducing us to a superior region of universal truths begins now to strike us as remote, uninteresting and unimportant. Reason, as a Kantian faculty that introduces generality and regularity into experience, strikes us more and more as superfluous—the unnecessary creation of men addicted to traditional formalism and to elaborate terminology. Concrete suggestions arising from past experiences, developed and matured in the light of the needs and deficiencies of the present, employed as aims and methods of specific reconstruction, and tested by success or failure in accomplishing this task of readjustment, suffice. To such empirical suggestions used in constructive fashion for new ends the name intelligence is given.

This recognition of the place of active and planning thought within the very processes of experience radically alters the traditional status of the technical problems of particular and universal, sense and reason, perceptual and conceptual. But the alteration is of much more than technical significance. For reason is experimental intelligence, conceived after the pattern of science, and used in the creation of social arts; it has something to do. It liberates man from the bondage of the past, due to ignorance and accident hardened into custom. It projects a better future and assists man in its realization. And its operation is always subject to test in experience. The plans which are formed, the principles which man projects as guides of reconstructive action, are not dogmas. They are hypotheses to be worked out in practice, and to be rejected, corrected and expanded as they fail or succeed in giving our present experience the guidance it requires. We may call them programmes of action, but since they are to be used in making our future acts less blind, more directed, they are flexible. Intelligence is not something possessed once for all. It is in constant process of forming, and its retention requires constant alertness in observing consequences, an open-minded will to learn and courage in re-adjustment.

In contrast with this experimental and re-adjusting intelligence, it must be said that Reason as employed by historic rationalism has tended to carelessness, conceit, irresponsibility, and rigidity—in short absolutism. A certain school of contemporary psychology uses the term " rationalization " to denote those mental mechanisms by which we unconsciously put a better face on our conduct or experience than facts justify. We excuse ourselves to ourselves by introducing a purpose and order into that of which we are secretly ashamed. In like fashion, historic rationalism has often tended to use Reason as an agency of justification and apologetics. It has taught that the defects and evils of actual experience disappear in the " rational whole " of things ; that things *appear* evil merely because of the partial, incomplete nature of experience. Or, as was noted by Bacon, " reason " assumes a false simplicity, uniformity and universality, and opens for science a path of fictitious ease. This course results in intellectual irresponsibility and neglect :—irresponsibility because rationalism assumes that the concepts of reason are so self-sufficient and so far above experience that they need and can secure no confirmation in experience. Neglect, because this same assumption makes men careless about concrete observations and experiments. Contempt for experience has had a tragic revenge *in* experience; it has cultivated disregard for fact and this disregard has been paid for in failure, sorrow and war.

The dogmatic rigidity of Rationalism is best seen in the consequences of Kant's attempt to buttress an otherwise chaotic experience with pure concepts. He set out with a laudable attempt at restricting the extravagant pretensions of Reason apart from experience. He called his philosophy critical. But because he taught that the understanding employs fixed, *a priori*, concepts, in order to introduce connection into experience and thereby make known *objects* possible (stable, regular relationships of qualities), he developed in German thought a curious contempt for the living variety of experience and a curious overestimate of the value of system, order, regularity for their own sakes. More practical causes were at work in producing the peculiarly German regard for drill, discipline, " order " and docility.

But Kant's philosophy served to provide an intellectual justification or " rationalization " of subordination of individuals to fixed and ready-made universals, " principles," laws. Reason and law were held to be synonyms. And as reason came into experience from without and above, so law had to come into life from some external and superior authority. The practical correlate to absolutism is rigidity, stiffness, inflexibility of disposition. When Kant taught that some conceptions, and these the important ones, are *a priori*, that they do not arise in experience and cannot be verified or tested in experience, that without such ready-made injections into experience the latter is anarchic and chaotic, he fostered the spirit of absolutism, even though technically he denied the possibility of absolutes. His successors were true to his spirit rather than his letter, and so they taught absolutism systematically. That the Germans with all their scientific competency and technological proficiency should have fallen into their tragically rigid and " superior " style of thought and action (tragic because involving them in inability to understand the world in which they lived) is a sufficient lesson of what may be involved in a systematical denial of the experimental character of intelligence and its conceptions.

By common consent, the effect of English empiricism was sceptical where that of German rationalism was apologetic; it undermined where the latter justified. It detected accidental associations formed into customs under the influence of self- or class-interest where German rational-idealism discovered profound meanings due to the necessary evolution of absolute reason. The modern world has suffered because in so many matters philosophy has offered it only an arbitrary choice between hard and fast opposites: Disintegrating analysis *or* rigid synthesis; complete radicalism neglecting and attacking the historic past as trivial and harmful, *or* complete conservatism idealizing institutions as embodiments of eternal reason; a resolution of experience into atomic elements that afford no support to stable organization *or* a clamping down of all experience by fixed categories and necessary concepts—these are the alternatives that conflicting schools have presented.

They are the logical consequences of the traditional opposition of Sense and Thought, Experience and Reason. Common sense has refused to follow both theories to their ultimate logic, and has fallen back on faith, intuition or the exigencies of practical compromise. But common sense too often has been confused and hampered instead of enlightened and directed by the philosophies proffered it by professional intellectuals. Men who are thrown back upon " common sense " when they appeal to philosophy for some general guidance are likely to fall back on routine, the force of some personality, strong leadership or on the pressure of momentary circumstances. It would be difficult to estimate the harm that has resulted because the liberal and progressive movement of the eighteenth and earlier nineteenth centuries had no method of intellectual articulation commensurate with its practical aspirations. Its heart was in the right place. It was humane and social in intention. But it had no theoretical instrumentalities of constructive power. Its head was sadly deficient. Too often the logical import of its professed doctrines was almost anti-social in their atomistic individualism, anti-human in devotion to brute sensation. This deficiency played into the hands of the reactionary and obscurantist. The strong point of the appeal to fixed principles transcending experience, to dogmas incapable of experimental verification, the strong point of reliance upon *a priori* canons of truth and standards of morals in opposition to dependence upon fruits and consequences in experience, has been the unimaginative conception of experience which professed philosophic empiricists have entertained and taught.

A philosophic reconstruction which should relieve men of having to choose between an impoverished and truncated experience on one hand and an artificial and impotent reason on the other would relieve human effort from the heaviest intellectual burden it has to carry. It would destroy the division of men of good will into two hostile camps. It would permit the co-operation of those who respect the past and the institutionally established with those who are interested in establishing a freer and happier future. For it would determine the conditions under which the funded experience of the past and the contriving intelligence which looks to the future can effectually interact with each other. It would enable men to glorify the claims of reason without at the same time falling into a paralyzing worship of super-empirical authority or into an offensive " rationalization " of things as they are.

CHAPTER V

CHANGED CONCEPTIONS OF THE IDEAL AND THE REAL

It has been noted that human experience is made human through the existence of associations and recollections, which are strained through the mesh of imagination so as to suit the demands of the emotions. A life that is humanly interesting is, short of the results of discipline, a life in which the tedium of vacant leisure is filled with images that excite and satisfy. It is in this sense that poetry preceded prose in human experience, religion antedated science, and ornamental and decorative art while it could not take the place of utility early reached a development out of proportion to the practical arts. In order to give contentment and delight, in order to feed present emotion and give the stream of conscious life intensity and color, the suggestions which spring from past experiences are worked over so as to smooth out their unpleasantnesses and enhance their enjoyableness. Some psychologists claim that there is what they call a natural tendency to obliviscence of the disagreeable—that men turn from the unpleasant in thought and recollection as they do

from the obnoxious in action. Every serious-minded
person knows that a large part of the effort required in
moral discipline consists in the courage needed to
acknowledge the unpleasant consequences of one's past
and present acts. We squirm, dodge, evade, disguise,
cover up, find excuses and palliations—anything to
render the mental scene less uncongenial. In short, the
tendency of spontaneous suggestion is to idealize experience, to give it in consciousness qualities which it
does not have in actuality. Time and memory are true
artists; they remould reality nearer to the heart's
desire.

As imagination becomes freer and less controlled by
concrete actualities, the idealizing tendency takes further flights unrestrained by the rein of the prosaic
world. The things most emphasized in imagination as
it reshapes experience are things which are absent in
reality. In the degree in which life is placid and easy,
imagination is sluggish and bovine. In the degree in
which life is uneasy and troubled, fancy is stirred to
frame pictures of a contrary state of things. By
reading the characteristic features of any man's castles
in the air you can make a shrewd guess as to his underlying desires which are frustrated. What is difficulty
and disappointment in real life becomes conspicuous
achievement and triumph in revery; what is negative in
fact will be positive in the image drawn by fancy; what

is vexation in conduct will be compensated for in high relief in idealizing imagination.

These considerations apply beyond mere personal psychology. They are decisive for one of the most marked traits of classic philosophy:—its conception of an ultimate supreme Reality which is essentially ideal in nature. Historians have more than once drawn an instructive parallel between the developed Olympian Pantheon of Greek religion and the Ideal Realm of Platonic philosophy. The gods, whatever their origin and original traits, became idealized projections of the selected and matured achievements which the Greeks admired among their mortal selves. The gods were like mortals, but mortals living only the lives which men would wish to live, with power intensified, beauty perfected, and wisdom ripened. When Aristotle criticized the theory of Ideas of his master, Plato, by saying that the Ideas were after all only things of sense eternalized, he pointed out in effect the parallelism of philosophy with religion and art to which allusion has just been made. And save for matters of merely technical import, is it not possible to say of Aristotle's Forms just what he said of Plato's Ideas? What are they, these Forms and Essences which so profoundly influenced for centuries the course of science and theology, save the objects of ordinary experience with their blemishes removed, their imperfections eliminated, their lacks

rounded out, their suggestions and hints fulfilled?
What are they in short but the objects of familiar life
divinized because reshaped by the idealizing imagination to meet the demands of desire in just those respects
in which actual experience is disappointing?

That Plato, and Aristotle in somewhat different
fashion, and Plotinus and Marcus Aurelius and Saint
Thomas Aquinas, and Spinoza and Hegel all taught
that Ultimate Reality is either perfectly Ideal and
Rational in nature, or else has absolute ideality and
rationality as its necessary attribute, are facts well
known to the student of philosophy. They need no ex-
position here. But it is worth pointing out that these
great systematic philosophies defined perfect Ideality
in conceptions that express the opposite of those things
which make life unsatisfactory and troublesome. What
is the chief source of the complaint of poet and moralist
with the goods, the values and satisfactions of experience? Rarely is the complaint that such things do not
exist; it is that although existing they are momentary,
transient, fleeting. They do not stay; at worst they
come only to annoy and tease with their hurried and dis-
appearing taste of what might be; at best they come
only to inspire and instruct with a passing hint of truer
reality. This commonplace of the poet and moralist
as to the impermanence not only of sensuous enjoyment, but of fame and civic achievements was profoundly

reflected upon by philosophers, especially by Plato and
Aristotle.   The results of their thinking have been
wrought into the very fabric of western ideas.   Time,
change, movement are signs that what the Greeks called
Non-Being somehow infect true Being.   The phrase-
ology is now strange, but many a modern who ridicules
the conception of Non-Being repeats the same thought
under the name of the Finite or Imperfect.

Wherever there is change, there is instability, and instability is proof of something the matter, of absence,
deficiency, incompleteness.   These are the ideas common to the connection between change, becoming and
perishing, and Non-Being, finitude and imperfection.
Hence complete and true Reality must be changeless,
unalterable, so full of Being that it always and forever maintains itself in fixed rest and repose.   As
Bradley, the most dialectially ingenious Absolutist of
our own day, expresses the doctrine " Nothing that is
perfectly real moves."   And while Plato took, comparatively speaking, a pessimistic view of change as mere
lapse and Aristotle a complacent view of it as tendency
to realization, yet Aristotle doubted no more than Plato
that the fully realized reality, the divine and ultimate, is
changeless.   Though it is called Activity or Energy, the
Activity knew no change, the energy did nothing.   It
was the activity of an army forever marking time and
never going anywhere.

From this contrast of the permanent with the transient arise other features which mark off the Ultimate Reality from the imperfect realities of practical life. Where there is change, there is of necessity numerical plurality, multiplicity, and from variety comes opposition, strife. Change is alteration, or " othering " and this means diversity. Diversity means division, and division means two sides and their conflict. The world which is transient *must* be a world of discord, for in lacking stability it lacks the government of unity. Did unity completely rule, these would remain an unchanging totality. What alters has parts and partialities which, not recognizing the rule of unity, assert themselves independently and make life a scene of contention and discord. Ultimate and true Being on the other hand, since it is changeless is Total, All-Comprehensive and One. Since it is One, it knows only harmony, and therefore enjoys complete and eternal Good. It *is* Perfection.

Degrees of knowledge and truth correspond with degrees of reality point by point. The higher and more complete the Reality the truer and more important the knowledge that refers to it. Since the world of becoming, of origins and perishings, is deficient in true Being, it cannot be known in the best sense. To know it means to neglect its flux and alteration and discover some permanent form which limits the processes that alter in time. The acorn undergoes a series of changes; these are knowable only in reference to the fixed form of the oak which is the same in the entire oak species in spite of the numerical diversity of trees. Moreover, this form limits the flux of growth at both ends, the acorn coming from the oak as well as passing into it. Where such unifying and limiting eternal forms cannot be detected, there is mere aimless variation and fluctuation, and knowledge is out of the question. On the other hand, as objects are approached in which there is no movement at all, knowledge becomes really demonstrative, certain, perfect—truth pure and unalloyed. The heavens can be more truly known than the earth, God the unmoved mover than the heavens.

From this fact follows the superiority of contemplative to practical knowledge, of pure theoretical speculation to experimentation, and to any kind of knowing that depends upon changes in things or that induces change in them. Pure knowing is pure beholding, viewing, noting. It is complete in itself. It looks for nothing beyond itself; it lacks nothing and hence has no aim or purpose. It is most emphatically its own excuse for being. Indeed, pure contemplative knowing is so much the most truly self-enclosed and self-sufficient thing in the universe that it is the highest and indeed the only attribute that can be ascribed to God, the Highest Being in the scale of Being. Man himself is divine in the rare moments when he attains to purely self-sufficient theoretical insight.

In contrast with such knowing, the so-called knowing of the artisan is base. He has to bring about changes in things, in wood and stone, and this fact is of itself evidence that his material is deficient in Being. What condemns his knowledge even more is the fact that it is not disinterestedly for its own sake. It has reference to results to be attained, food, clothing, shelter, etc. It is concerned with things that perish, the body and its needs. It thus has an ulterior aim, and one which itself testifies to imperfection. For want, desire, affection of every sort, indicate lack. Where there is need and desire—as in the case of all practical knowledge and activity—there is incompleteness and insufficiency. While civic or political and moral knowledge rank higher than do the conceptions of the artisan, yet intrinsically considered they are a low and untrue type. Moral and political action is practical; that is, it implies needs and effort to satisfy them. It has an end beyond itself. Moreover, the very fact of association shows lack of self-sufficiency; it shows dependence upon others. Pure knowing is alone solitary, and capable of being carried on in complete, self-sufficing independence.

In short, the measure of the worth of knowledge according to Aristotle, whose views are here summarized, is the degree in which it is purely contemplative. The highest degree is attained in knowing ultimate Ideal Being, pure Mind. This is Ideal, the Form of Forms, because it has no lacks, no needs, and experiences no change or variety. It has no desires because in it all desires are consummated. Since it is perfect Being, it is perfect Mind and perfect Bliss;—the acme of rationality and ideality. One point more and the argument is completed. The kind of knowing that concerns itself with this ultimate reality (which is also ultimate ideality) is philosophy. Philosophy is therefore the last and highest term in pure contemplation. Whatever may be said for any other kind of knowledge, philosophy is self-enclosed. It has nothing to do beyond itself; it has no aim or purpose or function—except to be philosophy—that is, pure, self-sufficing beholding of ultimate reality. There is of course such a thing as philosophic *study* which falls short of this perfection. Where there is learning, there is change and becoming. But the function of study and learning of philosophy is, as Plato put it, to convert the eye of the soul from dwelling contentedly upon the images of things, upon the inferior realities that are born and that decay, and to lead it to the intuition of supernal and eternal Being. Thus the mind of the knower is transformed. It becomes assimilated to what it knows.

Through a variety of channels, especially Neo-Platonism and St. Augustine, these ideas found their way into Christian theology; and great scholastic thinkers taught that the end of man is to know True Being, that knowledge is contemplative, that True Being is pure Immaterial Mind, and to know it is Bliss and Salvation. While this knowledge cannot be achieved in this stage of life nor without supernatural aid, yet so far as it is accomplished it assimilates the human mind to the divine essence and so constitutes salvation. Through this taking over of the conception of knowledge as Contemplative into the dominant religion of Europe, multitudes were affected who were totally innocent of theoretical philosophy. There was bequeathed to generations of thinkers as an unquestioned axiom the idea that knowledge is intrinsically a mere beholding or viewing of reality—the spectator conception of knowledge. So deeply engrained was this idea that it prevailed for centuries after the actual progress of science had demonstrated that knowledge is power to transform the world, and centuries after the practice of effective knowledge had adopted the method of experimentation.

Let us turn abruptly from this conception of the measure of true knowledge and the nature of true philosophy to the existing practice of knowledge. Nowadays if a man, say a physicist or chemist, wants to know something, the last thing he does is merely to contemplate. He does not look in however earnest and prolonged way upon the object expecting that thereby he will detect its fixed and characteristic form. He does not expect any amount of such aloof scrutiny to reveal to him any secrets. He proceeds to *do* something, to bring some energy to bear upon the substance to see how it reacts; he places it under unusual conditions in order to induce some change. While the astronomer cannot change the remote stars, even he no longer merely gazes. If he cannot change the stars themselves, he can at least by lens and prism change their light as it reaches the earth; he can lay traps for discovering changes which would otherwise escape notice. Instead of taking an antagonistic attitude toward change and denying it to the stars because of their divinity and perfection, he is on constant and alert watch to find some change through which he can form an inference as to the formation of stars and systems of stars.

Change in short is no longer looked upon as a fall from grace, as a lapse from reality or a sign of imperfection of Being. Modern science no longer tries to find some fixed form or essence behind each process of change. Rather, the experimental method tries to break down apparent fixities and to induce changes. The form that remains unchanged to sense, the form of seed or tree, is regarded not as the key to knowledge of the thing, but as a wall, an obstruction to be broken down. Consequently the scientific man experiments with this and that agency applied to this and that condition until something begins to happen; until there is, as we say, something doing. He assumes that there is change going on all the time, that there is movement within each thing in seeming repose; and that since the process is veiled from perception the way to know it is to bring the thing into novel circumstances until change becomes evident. In short, the thing which is to be accepted and paid heed to is not what is originally given but that which emerges after the thing has been set under a great variety of circumstances in order to see how it behaves.

Now this marks a much more general change in the human attitude than perhaps appears at first sight. It signifies nothing less than that the world or any part of it as it presents itself at a given time is accepted or acquiesced in only as *material* for change. It is accepted precisely as the carpenter, say, accepts things as he finds them. If he took them as things to be observed and noted for their own sake, he never would be a carpenter. He would observe, describe, record the structures, forms and changes which things exhibit to him, and leave the matter there. If perchance some of the changes going on should present him with a shelter, so much the better. But what makes the carpenter a *builder* is the fact that he notes things not just as objects in themselves, but with reference to what he

wants to do to them and with them; to the end he
has in mind. Fitness to effect certain special changes
that he wishes to see accomplished is what concerns
him in the wood and stones and iron which he observes.
His attention is directed to the changes they undergo
and the changes they make other things undergo so that
he may select that combination of changes which will
yield him his desired result. It is only by these processes
of active manipulation of things in order to realize his
purpose that he discovers what the properties of things
are. If he foregoes his own purpose and in the name
of a meek and humble subscription to things as they
" really are " refuses to bend things as they " are "
to his own purpose, he not only never achieves his purpose but he never learns what the things themselves are.
They *are* what they can do and what can be done with
them,—things that can be found by deliberate trying.

The outcome of this idea of the right way to know
is a profound modification in man's attitude toward the
natural world. Under differing social conditions, the
older or classic conception sometimes bred resignation
and submission; sometimes contempt and desire to
escape; sometimes, notably in the case of the Greeks,
a keen esthetic curiosity which showed itself in acute
noting of all the traits of given objects. In fact, the
whole conception of knowledge as beholding and noting
is fundamentally an idea connected with esthetic enjoy-

ment and appreciation where the environment is beautiful and life is serene, and with esthetic repulsion and depreciation where life is troubled, nature morose and hard. But in the degree in which the active conception of knowledge prevails, and the environment is regarded as something that has to be changed in order to be truly known, men are imbued with courage, with what may almost be termed an aggressive attitude toward nature. The latter becomes plastic, something to be subjected to human uses. The moral disposition toward change is deeply modified. This loses its pathos, it ceases to be haunted with melancholy through suggesting only decay and loss. Change becomes significant of new possibilities and ends to be attained; it becomes prophetic of a better future. Change is associated with progress rather than with lapse and fall. Since changes are going on anyway, the great thing is to learn enough about them so that we be able to lay hold of them and turn them in the direction of our desires. Conditions and events are neither to be fled from nor passively acquiesced in; they are to be utilized and directed. They are either obstacles to our ends or else means for their accomplishment. In a profound sense knowing ceases to be contemplative and becomes practical.

Unfortunately men, educated men, cultivated men in particular, are still so dominated by the older conception of an aloof and self-sufficing reason and knowledge that they refuse to perceive the import of this doctrine. They think they are sustaining the cause of impartial, thorough-going and disinterested reflection when they maintain the traditional philosophy of intellectualism— that is, of knowing as something self-sufficing and self-enclosed. But in truth, historic intellectualism, the spectator view of knowledge, is a purely compensatory doctrine which men of an intellectual turn have built up to console themselves for the actual and social impotency of the calling of thought to which they are devoted. Forbidden by conditions and held back by lack of courage from making their knowledge a factor in the determination of the course of events, they have sought a refuge of complacency in the notion that knowing is something too sublime to be contaminated by contact with things of change and practice. They have transformed knowing into a morally irresponsible estheticism. The true import of the doctrine of the operative or practical character of knowing, of intelligence, is objective. It means that the structures and objects which science and philosophy set up in contrast to the things and events of concrete daily experience do not constitute a realm apart in which rational contemplation may rest satisfied; it means that they represent the selected obstacles, material means and ideal methods of giving direction to that change which is bound to occur anyway.

This change of human disposition toward the world does not mean that man ceases to have ideals, or ceases to be primarily a creature of the imagination. But it does signify a radical change in the character and function of the ideal realm which man shapes for himself. In the classic philosophy, the ideal world is essentially a haven in which man finds rest from the storms of life; it is an asylum in which he takes refuge from the troubles of existence with the calm assurance that it alone is supremely real. When the belief that knowledge is active and operative takes hold of men, the ideal realm is no longer something aloof and separate; it is rather that collection of imagined possibilities that stimulates men to new efforts and realizations. It still remains true that the troubles which men undergo are the forces that lead them to project pictures of a better state of things. But the picture of the better is shaped so that it may become an instrumentality of action, while in the classic view the Idea belongs ready-made in a noumenal world. Hence, it is only an object of personal aspiration or consolation, while to the modern, an idea is a suggestion of something to be done or of a way of doing.

An illustration will, perhaps, make the difference clear. Distance is an obstacle, a source of trouble. It separates friends and prevents intercourse. It isolates, and makes contact and mutual understanding difficult.

This state of affairs provokes discontent and restless-
ness; it excites the imagination to construct pictures of
a state of things where human intercourse is not in-
juriously affected by space. Now there are two ways
out. One way is to pass from a mere dream of some
heavenly realm in which distance is abolished and by
some magic all friends are in perpetual transparent
communication, to pass, I say, from some idle castle-
building to philosophic reflection. Space, distance, it
will then be argued, is merely phenomenal; or, in a more
modern version, subjective. It is not, metaphysically
speaking, real. Hence the obstruction and trouble it
gives is not after all " real " in the metaphysical sense
of reality. Pure minds, pure spirits, do not live in a
space world; for them distance is not. Their relationships in the true world are not in any way affected by
special considerations. Their intercommunication is
direct, fluent, unobstructed.

Does the illustration involve a caricature of ways of
philosophizing with which we are all familiar? But if
it is not an absurd caricature, does it not suggest that
much of what philosophies have taught about the ideal
and noumenal or superiorly real world, is after all, only
casting a dream into an elaborate dialectic form
through the use of a speciously scientific terminology?
Practically, the difficulty, the trouble, remains. Practically, however it may be " metaphysically," space is

still real:—it acts in a definite objectionable way. Again, man dreams of some better state of things. From troublesome fact he takes refuge in fantasy. But this time, the refuge does not remain a permanent and remote asylum.

The idea becomes a standpoint from which to examine existing occurrences and to see if there is not among them something which gives a hint of how communication at a distance can be effected, something to be utilized as a medium of speech at long range. The suggestion or fancy though still ideal is treated as a possibility capable of realization *in* the concrete natural world, not as a superior reality apart from that world. As such, it becomes a platform from which to scrutinize natural events. Observed from the point of view of this possibility, things disclose properties hitherto undetected. In the light of these ascertainments, the idea of some agency for speech at a distance becomes less vague and floating: it takes on positive form. This action and reaction goes on. The possibility or idea is employed as a method for observing actual existence; and in the light of what is discovered the possibility takes on concrete existence. It becomes less of a mere idea, a fancy, a wished-for possibility, and more of an actual fact. Invention proceeds, and at last we have the telegraph, the telephone, first through wires, and then with no artificial medium. The concrete environment is transformed in the desired direction; it is idealized in fact and not merely in fancy. The ideal is realized through its own use as a tool or method of inspection, experimentation, selection and combination of concrete natural operations.

Let us pause to take stock of results. The division of the world into two kinds of Being, one superior, accessible only to reason and ideal in nature, the other inferior, material, changeable, empirical, accessible to sense-observation, turns inevitably into the idea that knowledge is contemplative in nature. It assumes a contrast between theory and practice which was all to the disadvantage of the latter. But in the actual course of the development of science, a tremendous change has come about. When the practice of knowledge ceased to be dialectical and became experimental, knowing became preoccupied with changes and the test of knowledge became the ability to bring about certain changes. Knowing, for the experimental sciences, means a certain kind of intelligently conducted doing; it ceases to be contemplative and becomes in a true sense practical. Now this implies that philosophy, unless it is to undergo a complete break with the authorized spirit of science, must also alter its nature. It must assume a practical nature; it must become operative and experimental. And we have pointed out what an enormous change this transformation of philosophy entails in the two conceptions which have played the greatest rôle in historic philosophizing—the conceptions of the "real" and "ideal" respectively. The former ceases to be something ready-made and final; it becomes that which has to be accepted as the material of change, as the obstructions and the means of certain specific desired changes. The ideal and rational also ceased to be a separate ready-made world incapable of being used as a lever to transform the actual empirical world, a mere asylum from empirical deficiencies. They represent intelligently thought-out possibilities *of* the existent world which may be used as methods for making over and improving it.

Philosophically speaking, this is the great difference involved in the change from knowledge and philosophy as contemplative to operative. The change does not mean the lowering in dignity of philosophy from a lofty plane to one of gross utilitarianism. It signifies that the prime function of philosophy is that of rationalizing the *possibilities* of experience, especially collective human experience. The scope of this change may be realized by considering how far we are from accomplishing it. In spite of inventions which enable men to use the energies of nature for their purposes, we are still far from habitually treating knowledge as the method of active control of nature and of experience. We tend to think of it after the model of a spectator viewing a finished picture rather than after that of the artist producing the painting. Thus there arise all the questions of epistemology with which the technical student of philosophy is so familiar, and which have made modern philosophy in especial so remote from the understanding of the everyday person and from the results and processes of science. For these questions all spring from the assumption of a merely beholding mind on one side and a foreign and remote object to be viewed and noted on the other. They ask how a mind and world, subject and object, so separate and independent can by any possibility come into such relationship to each other as to make true knowledge possible. If knowing were habitually conceived of as active and operative, after the analogy of experiment guided by hypothesis, or of invention guided by the imagination of some possibility, it is not too much to say that the first effect would be to emancipate philosophy from all the epistemological puzzles which now perplex it. For these all arise from a conception of the relation of mind and world, subject and object, in knowing, which assumes that to know is to seize upon what is already in existence.

Modern philosophic thought has been so preoccupied with these puzzles of epistemology and the disputes between realist and idealist, between phenomenalist and absolutist, that many students are at a loss to know what would be left for philosophy if there were removed both the metaphysical task of distinguishing between the noumenal and phenomenal worlds and the epistemological task of telling how a separate subject can know an independent object.   But would not the elimination of these traditional problems permit philosophy to devote itself to a more fruitful and more needed task?   Would it not encourage philosophy to face the great social and moral defects and troubles from which humanity suffers, to concentrate its attention upon clearing up the causes and exact nature of these evils and upon developing a clear idea of better social possibilities; in short upon projecting an idea or ideal which, instead of expressing the notion of another world or some far-away unrealizable goal, would be used as a method of understanding and rectifying specific social ills?

This is a vague statement.   But note in the first place that such a conception of the proper province of philosophy where it is released from vain metaphysics and idle epistemology is in line with the origin of philosophy sketched in the first hour.   And in the second place, note how contemporary society, the world over, is in need of more general and fundamental enlightenment and guidance than it now possesses.   I have tried to show that a radical change of the conception of knowledge from contemplative to active is the inevitable result of the way in which inquiry and invention are now conducted.   But in claiming this, it must also be conceded, or rather asserted, that so far the change has influenced for the most part only the more technical side of human life. The sciences have created new industrial arts. Man's physical command of natural energies has been indefinitely multiplied. There is control of the sources of material wealth and prosperity. What would once have been miracles are now daily performed with steam and coal and electricity and air, and with the human body. But there are few persons optimistic enough to declare that any similar command of the forces which control man's social and moral welfare has been achieved.

Where is the moral progress that corresponds to our economic accomplishments? The latter is the direct fruit of the revolution that has been wrought in physical science. But where is there a corresponding human science and art? Not only has the improvement in the method of knowing remained so far mainly limited to technical and economic matters. but this progress has brought with it serious new moral disturbances. I need only cite the late war, the problem of capital and labor, the relation of economic classes, the fact that while the new science has achieved wonders in medicine and surgery, it has also produced and spread occasions for diseases and weaknesses. These considerations indicate to us how undeveloped are our politics, how crude and primitive our education, how passive and inert our morals. The causes remain which brought philosophy into existence as an attempt to find an intelligent substitute for blind custom and blind impulse as guides to life and conduct. The attempt has not been successfully accomplished. Is there not reason for believing that the release of philosophy from its burden of sterile metaphysics and sterile epistemology instead of depriving philosophy of problems and subject-matter would open a way to questions of the most perplexing and the most significant sort?

Let me specify one problem quite directly suggested by certain points in this lecture. It has been pointed out that the really fruitful application of the contemplative idea was not in science but in the esthetic field. It is difficult to imagine any high development of the fine arts except where there is curious and loving interest in forms and motions of the world quite irrespective of any use to which they may be put. And it is not too much to say that every people that has attained a high esthetic development has been a people in which the contemplative attitude has flourished—as the Greek, the Hindoo, the medieval Christian. On the other hand, the scientific attitude that has actually proved itself in scientific progress is, as has been pointed out, a practical attitude. It takes forms as disguises for hidden processes. Its interest in change is in what it leads to, what can be done with it, to what use it can be put.

While it has brought nature under control, there is something hard and aggressive in its attitude toward nature unfavorable to the esthetic enjoyment of the world. Surely there is no more significant question before the world than this question of the possibility and method of reconciliation of the attitudes of practical science and contemplative esthetic appreciation. Without the former, man will be the sport and victim of natural forces which he cannot use or control. Without the latter, mankind might become a race of economic monsters, restlessly driving hard bargains with nature and with one another, bored with leisure or capable of putting it to use only in ostentatious display and extravagant dissipation.

Like other moral questions, this matter is social and even political. The western peoples advanced earlier on the path of experimental science and its applications in control of nature than the oriental. It is not, I suppose wholly fanciful, to believe that the latter have embodied in their habits of life more of the contemplative, esthetic and speculatively religious temper, and the former more of the scientific, industrial and practical. This difference and others which have grown up around it is one barrier to easy mutual understanding, and one source of misunderstanding. The philosophy which, then, makes a serious effort to comprehend these respective attitudes in their relation and due balance, could hardly fail to promote the capacity of peoples to profit by one another's experience and to co-operate more effectually with one another in the tasks of fruitful culture.

Indeed, it is incredible that the question of the relation of the " real " and the " ideal " should ever have been thought to be a problem belonging distinctively to philosophy. The very fact that this most serious of all human issues has been taken possession of by philosophy is only another proof of the disasters that follow in the wake of regarding knowledge and intellect as something self-sufficient. Never have the " real " and the " ideal " been so clamorous, so self-assertive, as at the present time. And never in the history of the world have they been so far apart. The world war was carried on for purely ideal ends:—for humanity, justice and equal liberty for strong and weak alike. And it was carried on by realistic means of applied science, by high explosives, and bombing airplanes and blockading marvels of mechanism that reduced the world well nigh to ruin, so that the serious-minded are concerned for the perpetuity of those choice values we call civilization. The peace settlement is loudly proclaimed in the name of the ideals that stir man's deepest emotions, but with the most realistic attention to details of economic advantage distributed in proportion to physical power to create future disturbances.

It is not surprising that some men are brought to regard all idealism as a mere smoke-screen behind which the search for material profit may be more effectually carried on, and are converted to the materialistic interpretation of history. "Reality" is then conceived as physical force and as sensations of power, profit and enjoyment; any politics that takes account of other factors, save as elements of clever propaganda and for control of those human beings who have not become realistically enlightened, is based on illusions. But others are equally sure that the real lesson of the war is that humanity took its first great wrong step when it entered upon a cultivation of physical science and an application of the fruits of science to the improvement of the instruments of life—industry and commerce. They will sigh for the return of the day when, while the great mass died as they were born in animal fashion, the few elect devoted themselves not to science and the material decencies and comforts of existence but to "ideal" things, the things of the spirit.

Yet the most obvious conclusion would seem to be the impotency and the harmfulness of any and every ideal that is proclaimed wholesale and in the abstract, that is, as something in itself apart from the detailed concrete existences whose moving possibilities it embodies. The true moral would seem to lie in enforcing the tragedy of that idealism which believes in a spiritual world which exists in and by itself, and the tragic need for the most realistic study of forces and consequences, a study conducted in a more scientifically accurate and complete manner than that of the professed *Real-politik*. For it is not truly realistic or scientific to take short views, to sacrifice the future to immediate pressure, to ignore facts and forces that are disagreeable and to magnify the enduring quality of whatever falls in with immediate desire. It is false that the evils of the situation arise from absence of ideals; they spring from wrong ideals. And these wrong ideals have in turn their foundation in the absence in social matters of that methodic, systematic, impartial, critical, searching inquiry into " real " and operative conditions which we call science and which has brought man in the technical realm to the command of physical energies.

Philosophy, let it be repeated, cannot " solve " the problem of the relation of the ideal and the real. That is the standing problem of life. But it can at least lighten the burden of humanity in dealing with the problem by emancipating mankind from the errors which philosophy has itself fostered—the existence of conditions which are real apart from their movement into something new and different, and the existence of ideals, spirit and reason independent of the possibilities of the material and physical. For as long as humanity is committed to this radically false bias, it will walk forward with blinded eyes and bound limbs. And philosophy can effect, if it will, something more than this negative task. It can make it easier for mankind to take the right steps in action by making it clear that a sympathetic and integral intelligence brought to bear upon the observation and understanding of concrete social events and forces, can form ideals, that is aims, which shall not be either illusions or mere emotional compensations.

CHAPTER VI

THE SIGNIFICANCE OF LOGICAL RECONSTRUCTION

Logic—like philosophy itself—suffers from a curious oscillation. It is elevated into the supreme and legislative science only to fall into the trivial estate of keeper of such statements as A is A and the scholastic verses for the syllogistic rules. It claims power to state the laws of the ultimate structure of the universe, on the ground that it deals with the laws of thought which are the laws according to which Reason has formed the world. Then it limits its pretensions to laws of correct reasoning which is correct even though it leads to no matter of fact, or even to material falsity. It is regarded by the modern objective idealist as the adequate substitute for ancient ontological metaphysics; but others treat it as that branch of rhetoric which teaches proficiency in argumentation. For a time a superficial compromise equilibrium was maintained wherein the logic of formal demonstration which the Middle Ages extracted from Aristotle was supplemented by an inductive logic of discovery of truth that Mill extracted from the practice of scientific men. But students of German philosophy, of mathematics, and of psychology, no matter how much they attacked one another, have made common cause in attack upon the orthodox logics both of deductive proof and inductive discovery.

Logical theory presents a scene of chaos. There is little agreement as to its subject-matter, scope or purpose. This disagreement is not formal or nominal but affects the treatment of every topic. Take such a rudimentary matter as the nature of judgment. Reputable authority can be quoted in behalf of every possible permutation of doctrine. Judgment is the central thing in logic; and judgment is not logical at all, but personal and psychological. If logical, it is the primary function to which both conception and inference are subordinate; and it is an after-product from them. The distinction of subject and predicate is necessary, and it is totally irrelevant; or again, though it is found in some cases, it is not of great importance. Among those who hold that the subject-predicate relationship is essential, some hold that judgment is an analysis of something prior into them, and others assert that it is a synthesis of them into something else. Some hold that reality is always the subject of judgment, and others that " reality " is logically irrelevant. Among those who deny that judgment is the attribution of predicate to subject, who regard it as a relation of elements, some hold that the relation is "internal," some that it is "external," and others that it is sometimes one and sometimes the other.

Unless logic is a matter of some practical account, these contrarieties are so numerous, so extensive, and so irreconcilable that they are ludicrous. If logic is an affair of practical moment, then these inconsistencies are serious. They testify to some deep-lying cause of intellectual disagreement and incoherency. In fact, contemporary logical theory is the ground upon which all philosophical differences and disputes are gathered together and focussed. How does the modification in the traditional conception of the relation of experience and reason, the real and ideal affect logic?

It affects, in the first place, the nature of logic itself. If thought or intelligence is the means of intentional reconstruction of experience, then logic, as an account of the procedure of thought, is not purely formal. It is not confined to laws of formally correct reasoning apart from truth of subject-matter. Neither, on the contrary, is it concerned with the inherent thought structures of the universe, as Hegel's logic would have it; nor with the successive approaches of human thought to this objective thought structure as the logic of Lotze, Bosanquet, and other epistemological logicians would have it. If thinking is the way in which deliberate re-organization of experience is secured, then logic is such a clarified and systematized formulation of the procedures of thinking as will enable the desired reconstruction to go on more economically and efficiently. In language familiar to students, logic is both a science and an art; a science so far as it gives an organized and tested descriptive account of the way in which thought actually goes on; an art, so far as on the basis of this description it projects methods by which future thinking shall take advantage of the operations that lead to success and avoid those which result in failure.

Thus is answered the dispute whether logic is empirical or normative, psychological or regulative. It is both. Logic is based on a definite and executive supply of empirical material. Men have been thinking for ages. They have observed, inferred, and reasoned in all sorts of ways and to all kinds of results. Anthropology, the study of the origin of myth, legend and cult; linguistics and grammar; rhetoric and former logical compositions all tell us how men have thought and what have been the purposes and consequences of different kinds of thinking. Psychology, experimental and pathological, makes important contributions to our knowledge of how thinking goes on and to what effect. Especially does the record of the growth of the various sciences afford instruction in those concrete ways of inquiry and testing which have led men astray and which have proved efficacious. Each science from mathematics to history exhibits typical fallacious methods and typical efficacious methods in special subject-matters. Logical theory has thus a large, almost inexhaustible field of empirical study.

The conventional statement that experience only tells us how men have thought or *do* think, while logic is concerned with norms, with how men *should* think, is ludicrously inept. Some sorts of thinking are shown *by* experience to have got nowhere, or worse than nowhere —into systematized delusion and mistake. Others have proved in manifest experience that they lead to fruitful and enduring discoveries. It is precisely in experience that the different consequences of different methods of investigation and ratiocination are convincingly shown. The parrot-like repetition of the distinction between an empirical description of what is and a normative account of what should be merely neglects the most striking fact about thinking as it empirically is— namely, its flagrant exhibition of cases of failure and success—that is, of good thinking and bad thinking. Any one who considers this empirical manifestation will not complain of lack of material from which to construct a *regulative* art. The more study that is given to empirical records of actual thought, the more apparent becomes the connection between the specific features of thinking which have produced failure and success. Out of this relationship of cause and effect as it is empirically ascertained grow the norms and regulations of an art of thinking.

Mathematics is often cited as an example of purely normative thinking dependent upon *a priori* canons and supra-empirical material. But it is hard to see how the student who approaches the matter historically can avoid the conclusion that the status of mathematics is as empirical as that of metallurgy. Men began with counting and measuring things just as they began with pounding and burning them. One thing, as common speech profoundly has it, led to another. Certain ways were successful—not merely in the immediately practical sense, but in the sense of being interesting, of arousing attention, of exciting attempts at improvement. The present-day mathematical logician may present the structure of mathematics as if it had sprung all at once from the brain of a Zeus whose anatomy is that of pure logic. But, nevertheless, this very structure is a product of long historic growth, in which all kinds of experiments have been tried, in which some men have struck out in this direction and some in that, and in which some exercises and operations have resulted in confusion and others in triumphant clarifications and fruitful growths; a history in which matter and methods have been constantly selected and worked over on the basis of empirical success and failure.

The structure of alleged normative *a priori* mathematics is in truth the crowned result of ages of toilsome experience. The metallurgist who should write on the most highly developed method of dealing with ores would not, in truth, proceed any differently. He too selects, refines, and organizes the methods which in the past have been found to yield the maximum of achievement. Logic is a matter of profound human importance precisely because it is empirically founded and experimentally applied. So considered, the problem of logical theory is none other than the problem of the possibility of the development and employment of intelligent method in inquiries concerned with deliberate reconstruction of experience. And it is only saying again in more specific form what has been said in general form to add that while such a logic has been developed in respect to mathematics and physical science, intelligent method, logic, is still far to seek in moral and political affairs.

Assuming, accordingly, this idea of logic without argument, let us proceed to discuss some of its chief features. First, light is thrown by the *origin* of thinking upon a logic which shall be a method of intelligent guidance of experience. In line with what has already been said about experience being a matter primarily of behavior, a sensori-motor matter, is the fact that thinking takes its departure from specific conflicts in experience that occasion perplexity and trouble. Men do not,

in their natural estate, think when they have no troubles
to cope with, no difficulties to overcome. A life of ease,
of success without effort, would be a thoughtless life,
and so also would a life of ready omnipotence. Beings who think are beings whose life is so hemmed in
and constricted that they cannot directly carry through
a course of action to victorious consummation. Men
also do not tend to think when their action, when they
are amid difficulties, is dictated to them by authority.
Soldiers have difficulties and restrictions in plenty, but
qua soldiers (as Aristotle would say) they are not no-
torious for being thinkers. Thinking is done for them,
higher up. The same is too true of most workingmen
under present economic conditions. Difficulties occasion
thinking only when thinking is the imperative or urgent
way out, only when it is the indicated road to a solution. Wherever external authority reigns, thinking is
suspected and obnoxious.

Thinking, however, is not the only way in which a
personal solution of difficulties is sought. As we have
seen, dreams, reveries, emotional idealizations are roads
which are taken to escape the strain of perplexity and
conflict. According to modern psychology, many systematized delusions and mental disorders, probably hys-
teria itself, originate as devices for getting freedom
from troublesome conflicting factors. Such considerations throw into relief some of the traits essential to

thinking as a way of responding to difficulty. The short-cut " solutions " alluded to do not get rid of the conflict and problems; they only get rid of the feeling of it. They cover up consciousness of it. Because the conflict remains in fact and is evaded in thought, disorders arise.

The first distinguishing characteristic of thinking then is facing the facts—inquiry, minute and extensive scrutinizing, observation. Nothing has done greater harm to the successful conduct of the enterprise of thinking (and to the logics which reflect and formulate the undertaking) than the habit of treating observation as something outside of and prior to thinking, and thinking as something which can go on in the head without *including* observation of new facts as part of itself. Every approximation to such " thinking " is really an approach to the method of escape and self-delusion just referred to. It substitutes an emotionally agreeable and rationally self-consistent train of meanings for inquiry into the features of the situation which cause the trouble. It leads to that type of Idealism which has well been termed intellectual somnambulism. It creates a class of " thinkers " who are remote from practice and hence from testing their thought by application—a socially superior and irresponsible class. This is the condition causing the tragic division of theory and practice, and leading to an unreasonable exaltation of theory on one side and an unreasonable contempt for it on the other. It confirms current practice in its hard brutalities and dead routines just because it has transferred thinking and theory to a separate and nobler region. Thus has the idealist conspired with the materialist to keep actual life impoverished and inequitable.

The isolation of thinking from confrontation with facts encourages that kind of observation which merely accumulates brute facts, which occupies itself laboriously with mere details, but never inquires into their meaning and consequences—a safe occupation, for it never contemplates any use to be made of the observed facts in determining a plan for changing the situation. Thinking which is a method of reconstructing experience treats observation of facts, on the other hand, as the indispensable step of defining the problem, of locating the trouble, of forcing home a definite, instead of a merely vague emotional, sense of what the difficulty is and where it lies. It is not aimless, random, miscellaneous, but purposeful, specific and limited by the character of the trouble undergone. The purpose is so to clarify the disturbed and confused situation that reasonable ways of dealing with it may be suggested. When the scientific man appears to observe aimlessly, it is merely that he is so in love with problems as sources and guides of inquiry, that he is striving to turn up a problem where none appears on the surface: he is, as we say, hunting for trouble because of the satisfaction to be had in coping with it.

Specific and wide observation of concrete fact always, then, corresponds not only with a sense of a problem or difficulty, but with some vague sense of the *meaning* of the difficulty, that is, of what it imports or signifies in subsequent experience. It is a kind of anticipation or prediction of what is coming. We speak, very truly, of *impending* trouble, and in observing the signs of what the trouble is, we are at the same time expecting, forecasting—in short, framing an *idea*, becoming aware of meaning. When the trouble is not only impending but completely actual and present, we are overwhelmed. We do not think, but give way to depression. The kind of trouble that occasions thinking is that which is incomplete and developing, and where what is found already in existence can be employed as a sign from which to infer what is likely to come. When we intelligently observe, we are, as we say apprehensive, as well as apprehending. We are on the alert for something still to come. Curiosity, inquiry, investigation, are directed quite as truly into what is going to happen next as into what has happened. An intelligent interest in the latter is an interest in getting evidence, indications, symptoms for inferring the former. Observation is diagnosis and diagnosis implies an interest in anticipation and preparation. It makes ready in advance an attitude of response so that we shall not be caught unawares.

That which is not already in existence, that which is only anticipated and inferred, cannot be observed. It does not have the status of fact, of something given, a datum, but of a meaning, an idea. So far as ideas are not fancies, framed by emotionalized memory for escape and refuge, they are precisely anticipations of something still to come aroused by looking into the facts of a developing situation. The blacksmith watches his iron, its color and texture, to get evidence of what it is getting ready to pass into; the physician observes his patient to detect symptoms of change in some definite direction; the scientific man keeps his attention upon his laboratory material to get a clue as to what *will* happen under certain conditions. The very fact that observation is not an end in itself but a search for evidence and signs shows that along with observation goes inference, anticipatory forecast—in short an idea, thought or conception.

In a more technical context, it would be worth while to see what light this logical correspondence of observed fact and projected idea or meaning throws upon certain traditional philosophical problems and puzzles, including that of subject and predicate in judgment, object and subject in knowledge, " real " and " ideal " generally. But at this time, we must confine ourselves to pointing out that this view of the correlative origin and function of observed fact and projected idea in experience, commits us to some very important consequences concerning the nature of ideas, meanings, conceptions, or whatever word may be employed to denote the specifically *mental* function. Because they are suggestions of something that may happen or eventuate, they are (as we saw in the case of ideals generally) platforms of response to what is going on. The man who detects that the cause of his difficulty is an automobile bearing down upon him is not guaranteed safety; he may have made his observation-forecast too late. But if his anticipation-perception comes in season, he has the basis for doing something which will avert threatening disaster. Because he foresees an impending result, he may do something that will lead to the situation eventuating in some other way. All intelligent thinking means an increment of freedom in action—an emancipation from chance and fatality. " Thought " represents the suggestion of a way of response that is different from that which would have been followed if intelligent observation had not effected an inference as to the future.

Now a method of action, a mode of response, intended to produce a certain result—that is, to enable the blacksmith to give a certain form to his hot iron, the physician to treat the patient so as to facilitate recovery, the scientific experimenter to draw a conclusion which will apply to other cases,—is by the nature of the case tentative, uncertain till tested by its results. The significance of this fact for the theory of truth will be discussed below. Here it is enough to note that notions, theories, systems, no matter how elaborate and self-consistent they are, must be regarded as hypotheses. They are to be accepted as bases of actions which test them, not as finalities. To perceive this fact is to abolish rigid dogmas from the world. It is to recognize that conceptions, theories and systems of thought are always open to development through use. It is to enforce the lesson that we must be on the lookout quite as much for indications to alter them as for opportunities to assert them. They are tools. As in the case of all tools, their value resides not in themselves but in their capacity to work shown in the consequences of their use.

Nevertheless, inquiry is free only when the interest in knowing is so developed that thinking carries with it something worth while for itself, something having its own esthetic and moral interest. Just because knowing is not self-enclosed and final but is instrumental to reconstruction of situations, there is always danger that it will be subordinated to maintaining some preconceived purpose or prejudice. Then reflection ceases to be complete; it falls short. Being precommitted to arriving at some special result, it is not sincere. It is one thing to say that all knowing has an end beyond itself, and another thing, a thing of a contrary kind, to say that an act of knowing has a particular end which it is bound, in advance, to reach. Much less is it true that the instrumental nature of thinking means that it exists for the sake of attaining some private, one-sided advantage upon which one has set one's heart. Any limitation whatever of the end means limitation in the thinking process itself. It signifies that it does not attain its full growth and movement, but is cramped, impeded, interfered with. The only situation in which knowing is fully stimulated is one in which the end is developed in the process of inquiry and testing.

Disinterested and impartial inquiry is then far from meaning that knowing is self-enclosed and irresponsible. It means that there is no particular end set up in advance so as to shut in the activities of observation, forming of ideas, and application. Inquiry is emancipated. It is encouraged to attend to every fact that is relevant to defining the problem or need, and to follow up every suggestion that promises a clue. The barriers to free inquiry are so many and so solid that mankind is to be congratulated that the very act of investigation is capable of itself becoming a delightful and absorbing pursuit, capable of enlisting on its side man's sporting instincts.

Just in the degree in which thought ceases to be held down to ends fixed by social custom, a social division of labor grows up. Investigation has become a dominant life occupation for some persons. Only superficially, however, does this confirm the idea that theory and knowledge are ends in themselves. They are, relatively speaking, ends in themselves for some persons. But these persons represent a social division of labor; and their specialization can be trusted only when such persons are in unobstructed co-operation with other social occupations, sensitive to others' problems and transmitting results to them for wider application in action. When this social relationship of persons particularly engaged in carrying on the enterprise of knowing is forgotten and the class becomes isolated, inquiry loses stimulus and purpose. It degenerates into sterile specialization, a kind of intellectual busy work carried on by socially absent-minded men. Details are heaped up in the name of science, and abstruse dialectical developments of systems occur. Then the occupation is "rationalized" under the lofty name of devotion to truth for its own sake. But when the path of true science is retaken these things are brushed aside and forgotten. They turn out to have been the toyings of vain and irresponsible men. The only guarantee of impartial, disinterested inquiry is the social sensitiveness of the inquirer to the needs and problems of those with whom he is associated.

As the instrumental theory is favorable to high esteem for impartial and disinterested inquiry, so, contrary to the impressions of some critics, it sets much store upon the apparatus of deduction. It is a strange notion that because one says that the cognitive value of conceptions, definitions, generalizations, classifications and the development of consecutive implications is not self-resident, that therefore one makes light of the deductive function, or denies its fruitfulness and necessity. The instrumental theory only attempts to state with some scrupulousness *where* the value is found and to prevent its being sought in the wrong place. It says that knowing begins with specific observations that define the problem and ends with specific observations that test a hypothesis for its solution. But that the idea, the meaning, which the original observations suggest and the final ones test, itself requires careful scrutiny and prolonged development, the theory would be the last to deny. To say that a locomotive is an agency, that it is intermediate between a need in experience and its satisfaction, is not to depreciate the worth of careful and elaborate construction of the locomotive, or the need of subsidiary tools and processes that are devoted to introducing improvements into its structure. One would rather say that *because* the locomotive is intermediary in experience, not primary and not final, it is impossible to devote too much care to its constructive development.

Such a deductive science as mathematics represents the perfecting of method. That a method to those concerned with it should present itself as an end on its own account is no more surprising than that there should be a distinct business for making any tool. Rarely are those who invent and perfect a tool those who employ it. There is, indeed, one marked difference between the physical and the intellectual instrumentality. The development of the latter runs far beyond any immediately visible use. The artistic interest in perfecting the method by itself is strong—as the utensils of civilization may themselves become works of finest art. But from the practical standpoint this difference shows that the advantage as an instrumentality is on the side of the intellectual tool. Just because it is not formed with a special application in mind, because it is a highly generalized tool, it is the more flexible in adaptation to unforeseen uses. It can be employed in dealing with problems that were not anticipated. The mind is prepared in advance for all sorts of intellectual emergencies, and when the new problem occurs it does not have to wait till it can get a special instrument ready.

More definitely, abstraction is indispensable if one

experience is to be applicable in other experiences. Every concrete experience in its totality is unique; it is itself, non-reduplicable. Taken in its full concreteness, it yields no instruction, it throws no light. What is called abstraction means that some phase of it is selected for the sake of the aid it gives in grasping something else. Taken by itself, it is a mangled fragment, a poor substitute for the living whole from which it is extracted. But viewed teleologically or practically, it represents the only way in which one experience can be made of any value for another—the only way in which something enlightening can be secured. What is called false or vicious abstractionism signifies that the *function* of the detached fragment is forgotten and neglected, so that it is esteemed barely in itself as something of a higher order than the muddy and irregular concrete from which it was wrenched. Looked at functionally, not structurally and statically, abstraction means that something has been released from one experience for transfer to another. Abstraction is liberation. The more theoretical, the more abstract, an abstraction, or the farther away it is from anything experienced in its concreteness, the better fitted it is to deal with any one of the indefinite variety of things that may later present themselves. Ancient mathematics and physics were much nearer the gross concrete experience than are modern. For that very reason they were more impotent in affording any insight into and control over such concretes as present themselves in new and unexpected forms.

Abstraction and generalization have always been recognized as close kin. It may be said that they are the negative and positive sides of the same function. Abstraction sets free some factor so that it may be used. Generalization is the use. It carries over and extends. It is always in some sense a leap in the dark. It is an adventure. There can be no assurance in advance that what is extracted from one concrete can be fruitfully extended to another individual case. Since these other cases are individual and concrete they *must* be dissimilar. The trait of flying is detached from the concrete bird. This abstraction is then carried over to the bat, and it is expected in view of the application of the quality to have some of the other traits of the bird. This trivial instance indicates the essence of generalization, and also illustrates the riskiness of the proceeding. It transfers, extends, applies, a result of some former experience to the reception and interpretation of a new one. Deductive processes define, delimit, purify and set in order the conceptions through which this enriching and directive operation is carried on, but they cannot, however perfect, guarantee the outcome.

The pragmatic value of organization is so conspicuously enforced in contemporary life that it hardly seems necessary to dwell upon the instrumental significance of classification and systematization. When the existence of qualitative and fixed species was denied to be the supreme object of knowledge, classification was often regarded, especially by the empirical school, as merely a linguistic device. It was convenient for memory and communication to have words that sum up a number of particulars. Classes were supposed to exist only in speech. Later, ideas were recognized as a kind of *tertium quid* between things and words. Classes were allowed to exist in the mind as purely mental things. The critical disposition of empiricism is well exemplified here. To assign any objectivity to classes was to encourage a belief in eternal species and occult essences and to strengthen the arms of a decadent and obnoxious science—a point of view well illustrated in Locke. General *ideas* are useful in economizing effort, enabling us to condense particular experiences into simpler and more easily carried bunches and making it easier to identify new observations.

So far nominalism and conceptualism—the theory that kinds exist only in words or in ideas—was on the right track. It emphasized the teleological character of systems and classifications, that they exist for the sake of economy and efficiency in reaching ends. But this truth was perverted into a false notion, because

the active and doing side of experience was denied or
ignored. Concrete things have *ways* of acting, as many
ways of acting as they have points of interaction with
other things. One thing is callous, unresponsive, inert
in the presence of some other things; it is alert, eager,
and on the aggressive with respect to other things; in
a third case, it is receptive, docile. Now different ways
of behaving, in spite of their endless diversity, may be
classed together in view of common relationship to an
end. No sensible person tries to do everything. He
has certain main interests and leading aims by which
he makes his behavior coherent and effective. To have
an aim is to limit, select, concentrate, group. Thus a
basis is furnished for selecting and organizing things
according as their ways of acting are related to carrying forward pursuit. Cherry trees will be differently grouped by woodworkers, orchardists, artists,
scientists and merry-makers. To the execution of
different purposes different ways of acting and re-
acting on the part of trees are important. Each
classification may be equally sound when the difference
of ends is borne in mind.

Nevertheless there is a genuine objective standard for
the goodness of special classifications. One will further
the cabinetmaker in reaching his end while another will
hamper him. One classification will assist the botanist
in carrying on fruitfully his work of inquiry, and an-

other will retard and confuse him. The teleological theory of classification does not therefore commit us to the notion that classes are purely verbal or purely mental. Organization is no more merely nominal or mental in any art, including the art of inquiry, than it is in a department store or railway system. The necessity of execution supplies objective criteria. Things have to be sorted out and arranged so that their grouping will promote successful action for ends. Convenience, economy and efficiency are the bases of classification, but these things are not restricted to verbal communication with others nor to inner consciousness; they concern objective action. They must take effect in the world.

At the same time, a classification is not a bare transcript or duplicate of some finished and done-for arrangement pre-existing in nature. It is rather a repertory of weapons for attack upon the future and the unknown. For success, the details of past knowledge must be reduced from bare facts to meanings, the fewer, simpler and more extensive the better. They must be broad enough in scope to prepare inquiry to cope with any phenomenon however unexpected. They must be arranged so as not to overlap, for otherwise when they are applied to new events they interfere and produce confusion. In order that there may be ease and economy of movement in dealing with the

enormous diversity of occurrences that present themselves, we must be able to move promptly and definitely
from one tool of attack to another. In other words,
our various classes and kinds must be themselves classified in graded series from the larger to the more specific. There must not only be streets, but the streets
must be laid out with reference to facilitating passage
from any one to any other. Classification transforms
a wilderness of by-ways in experience into a well-
ordered system of roads, promoting transportation
and communication in inquiry. As soon as men begin
to take foresight for the future and to prepare themselves in advance to meet it effectively and prosper-
ously, the deductive operations and their results gain
in importance. In every practical enterprise there are
goods to be produced, and whatever eliminates wasted
material and promotes economy and efficiency of production is precious.

Little time is left to speak of the account of the
nature of truth given by the experimental and func-
tional type of logic. This is less to be regretted because this account is completely a corollary from the
nature of thinking and ideas. If the view held as to
the latter is understood, the conception of truth follows as a matter of course. If it be not understood,
any attempt to present the theory of truth is bound
to be confusing, and the theory itself to seem arbi-

trary and absurd. *If* ideas, meanings, conceptions,
notions, theories, systems are instrumental to an active
reorganization of the given environment, to a removal
of some specific trouble and perplexity, then the test of
their validity and value lies in accomplishing this work.
If they succeed in their office, they are reliable, sound,
valid, good, true. If they fail to clear up confusion,
to eliminate defects, if they increase confusion, uncertainty and evil when they are acted upon, then are they
false. Confirmation, corroboration, verification lie in
works, consequences. Handsome is that handsome does.
By their fruits shall ye *know* them. That which guides
us truly is true—demonstrated capacity for such guidance is precisely what is meant by truth.   The adverb
" truly " is more fundamental than either the adjec-
tive, true, or the noun, truth. An adverb expresses a
way, a mode of acting. Now an idea or conception is
a claim or injunction or plan to *act* in a certain way
as the way to arrive at the clearing up of a specific
situation. When the claim or pretension or plan is
acted upon *it guides us truly or falsely;* it leads us to
our end or away from it. Its active, dynamic function
is the all-important thing about it, and in the quality
of activity induced by it lies all its truth and falsity.
The hypothesis that works is the *true* one; and
truth is an abstract noun applied to the collection
of cases, actual, foreseen and desired, that

receive confirmation in their works and consequences.

So wholly does the worth of this conception of truth
depend upon the correctness of the prior account of
thinking that it is more profitable to consider why
the conception gives offence than to expound it on its
own account. Part of the reason why it has been
found so obnoxious is doubtless its novelty and defects
in its statement. Too often, for example, when truth
has been thought of as satisfaction, it has been thought
of as merely emotional satisfaction, a private comfort,
a meeting of purely personal need. But the satisfaction in question means a satisfaction of the needs and
conditions of the problem out of which the idea, the
purpose and method of action, arises. It includes
public and objective conditions. It is not to be manipulated by whim or personal idiosyncrasy. Again
when truth is defined as utility, it is often thought
to mean utility for some purely personal end, some
profit upon which a particular individual has set his
heart. So repulsive is a conception of truth which
makes it a mere tool of private ambition and ag-
grandizement, that the wonder is that critics have
attributed such a notion to sane men. As matter of
fact, truth as utility means service in making just that
contribution to reorganization in experience that the
idea or theory claims to be able to make. The usefulness

of a road is not measured by the degree in which it
lends itself to the purposes of a highwayman. It is
measured by whether it actually functions *as* a road, as
a means of easy and effective public transportation and
communication. And so with the serviceableness of an
idea or hypothesis as a measure of its truth.

Turning from such rather superficial misunderstand-
ings, we find, I think, the chief obstacle to the reception of this notion of truth in an inheritance from the
classic tradition that has become so deeply engrained in
men's minds. In just the degree in which existence is
divided into two realms, a higher one of perfect being
and a lower one of seeming, phenomenal, deficient
reality, truth and falsity are thought of as fixed, ready-
made static properties of things themselves. Supreme
Reality is true Being, inferior and imperfect Reality is
false Being. It makes claims to Reality which it cannot substantiate. It is deceitful, fraudulent, inherently
unworthy of trust and belief. Beliefs are false not because they mislead us; they are not mistaken ways of
thinking. They are false because they admit and ad-
here to false existences or subsistences. Other notions
are true because they do have to do with true Being—
with full and ultimate Reality. Such a notion lies at
the back of the head of every one who has, in however
an indirect way, been a recipient of the ancient and
medieval tradition. This view is radically challenged by

the pragmatic conception of truth, and the impossibility of reconciliation or compromise is, I think, the cause of the shock occasioned by the newer theory.

This contrast, however, constitutes the importance of the new theory as well as the unconscious obstruction to its acceptance. The older conception worked out practically to identify truth with authoritative dogma. A society that chiefly esteems order, that finds growth painful and change disturbing, inevitably seeks for a fixed body of superior truths upon which it may depend. It looks backward, to something already in existence, for the source and sanction of truth. It falls back upon what is antecedent, prior, original, *a priori*, for assurance. The thought of looking ahead, toward the eventual, toward consequences, creates uneasiness and fear. It disturbs the sense of rest that is attached to the ideas of fixed Truth already in existence. It puts a heavy burden of responsibility upon us for search, unremitting observation, scrupulous development of hypotheses and thoroughgoing testing. In physical matters men have slowly grown accustomed in all specific beliefs to identifying the true with the verified. But they still hesitate to recognize the implication of this identification and to derive the definition of truth from it. For while it is nominally agreed upon as a commonplace that definitions ought to spring from concrete and specific cases rather than be invented in the empty air and imposed upon particulars, there is a strange unwillingness to act upon the maxim in defining truth. To generalize the recognition that the true means the verified and means nothing else places upon men the responsibility for surrendering political and moral dogmas, and subjecting to the test of consequences their most cherished prejudices. Such a change involves a great change in the seat of authority and the methods of decision in society. Some of them, as first fruits of the newer logic, will be considered in the following lectures.

CHAPTER VII

RECONSTRUCTION IN MORAL CONCEPTIONS

THE impact of the alteration in methods of scientific thinking upon moral ideas is, in general, obvious. Goods, ends are multiplied. Rules are softened into principles, and principles are modified into methods of understanding. Ethical theory began among the Greeks as an attempt to find a regulation for the conduct of life which should have a rational basis and purpose instead of being derived from custom. But reason as a substitute for custom was under the obligation of supplying objects and laws as fixed as those of custom had been. Ethical theory ever since has been singularly hypnotized by the notion that its business is to discover some final end or good or some ultimate and supreme law. This is the common element among the diversity of theories. Some have held that the end is loyalty or obedience to a higher power or authority; and they have variously found this higher principle in Divine Will, the will of the secular ruler, the maintenance of institutions in which the purpose of superiors is embodied, and the rational consciousness of duty. But they have differed from one another because there was

one point in which they were agreed: a single and **final**
source of law. Others have asserted that it is impossible
to locate morality in conformity to law-giving power,
and that it must be sought in ends that are goods. And
some have sought the good in self-realization, some in
holiness, some in happiness, some in the greatest possible aggregate of pleasures. And yet these schools
have agreed in the assumption that there is a single,
fixed and final good. They have been able to dispute with one another only because of their common
premise.

The question arises whether the way out of the confusion and conflict is not to go to the root of the
matter by questioning this common element. Is not the
belief in the single, final and ultimate (whether conceived as good or as authoritative law) an intellectual
product of that feudal organization which is disappear-
ing historically and of that belief in a bounded, ordered
cosmos, wherein rest is higher than motion, which has
disappeared from natural science? It has been re-
peatedly suggested that the present limit of intellectual
reconstruction lies in the fact that it has not as yet
been seriously applied in the moral and social disci-
plines. Would not this further application demand
precisely that we advance to a belief in a plurality of
changing, moving, individualized goods and ends, and
to a belief that principles, criteria, laws are intellectual

instruments for analyzing individual or unique situations?

The blunt assertion that every moral situation is a unique situation having its own irreplaceable good may seem not merely blunt but preposterous. For the established tradition teaches that it is precisely the irregularity of special cases which makes necessary the guidance of conduct by universals, and that the essence of the virtuous disposition is willingness to subordinate every particular case to adjudication by a fixed principle. It would then follow that submission of a generic end and law to determination by the concrete situation entails complete confusion and unrestrained licentiousness. Let us, however, follow the pragmatic rule, and in order to discover the meaning of the idea ask for its consequences. Then it surprisingly turns out that the primary significance of the unique and morally ultimate character of the concrete situation is to transfer the weight and burden of morality to intelligence. It does not destroy responsibility; it only locates it. A moral situation is one in which judgment and choice are required antecedently to overt action. The practical meaning of the situation —that is to say the action needed to satisfy it—is not self-evident. It has to be searched for. There are conflicting desires and alternative apparent goods. What is needed is to find the right course of action, the right good. Hence, inquiry is exacted: observation of the detailed makeup of the situation; analysis into its diverse factors; clarification of what is obscure; discounting of the more insistent and vivid traits; tracing the consequences of the various modes of action that suggest themselves; regarding the decision reached as hypothetical and tentative until the anticipated or supposed consequences which led to its adoption have been squared with actual consequences. This inquiry is intelligence. Our moral failures go back to some weakness of disposition, some absence of sympathy, some one-sided bias that makes us perform the judgment of the concrete case carelessly or perversely. Wide sympathy, keen sensitiveness, persistence in the face of the disagreeable, balance of interests enabling us to undertake the work of analysis and decision intelligently are the distinctively moral traits—the virtues or moral excellencies.

It is worth noting once more that the underlying issue is, after all, only the same as that which has been already threshed out in physical inquiry. There too it long seemed as if rational assurance and demonstration could be attained only if we began with universal conceptions and subsumed particular cases under them. The men who initiated the methods of inquiry that are now everywhere adopted were denounced in their day (and sincerely) as subverters of truth and foes of science. If they have won in the end, it is because, as has already been pointed out, the method of universals confirmed prejudices and sanctioned ideas that had gained currency irrespective of evidence for them; while placing the initial and final weight upon the individual case, stimulated painstaking inquiry into facts and examination of principles. In the end, loss of eternal truths was more than compensated for in the accession of quotidian facts. The loss of the system of superior and fixed definitions and kinds was more than made up for by the growing system of hypotheses and laws used in classifying facts. After all, then, we are only pleading for the adoption in moral reflection of the logic that has been proved to make for security, stringency and fertility in passing judgments upon physical phenomena. And the reason is the same. The old method in spite of its nominal and esthetic worship of reason discouraged reason, because it hindered the operation of scrupulous and unremitting inquiry.

More definitely, the transfer of the burden of the moral life from following rules or pursuing fixed ends over to the detection of the ills that need remedy in a special case and the formation of plans and methods for dealing with them, eliminates the causes which have kept moral theory controversial, and which have also kept it remote from helpful contact with the exigencies of practice. The theory of fixed ends inevitably leads thought into the bog of disputes that cannot be settled. If there is one *summum bonum*, one supreme end, what is it? To consider this problem is to place ourselves in the midst of controversies that are as acute now as they were two thousand years ago. Suppose we take a seemingly more empirical view, and say that while there is not a single end, there also are not as many as there are specific situations that require amelioration; but there are a number of such natural goods as health, wealth, honor or good name, friendship, esthetic appreciation, learning and such moral goods as justice, temperance, benevolence, etc. What or who is to decide the right of way when these ends conflict with one another, as they are sure to do? Shall we resort to the method that once brought such disrepute upon the whole business of ethics: Casuistry? Or shall we have recourse to what Bentham well called the *ipse dixit* method: the arbitrary preference of this or that person for this or that end? Or shall we be forced to arrange them all in an order of degrees from the highest good down to the least precious? Again we find ourselves in the middle of unreconciled disputes with no indication of the way out.

Meantime, the special moral perplexities where the aid of intelligence is required go unenlightened. We cannot seek or attain health, wealth, learning, justice

or kindness in general. Action is always specific, concrete, individualized, unique. And consequently judgments as to acts to be performed must be similarly
specific. To say that a man seeks health or justice
is only to say that he seeks to live healthily or justly.
These things, like truth, are adverbial. They are modi-
fiers of action in special cases. How to live healthily
or justly is a matter which differs with every person.
It varies with his past experience, his opportunities, his
temperamental and acquired weaknesses and abilities.
Not man in general but a particular man suffering from
some particular disability aims to live healthily, and
consequently health cannot mean for him exactly what it
means for any other mortal. Healthy living is not something to be attained by itself apart from other ways of
living. A man needs to be healthy *in* his life, not apart
from it, and what does life mean except the aggregate
of his pursuits and activities? A man who aims at
health as a distinct end becomes a valetudinarian, or a
fanatic, or a mechanical performer of exercises, or an
athlete so one-sided that his pursuit of bodily development injures his heart. When the endeavor to
realize a so-called end does not temper and color all
other activities, life is portioned out into strips and
fractions. Certain acts and times are devoted to getting
health, others to cultivating religion, others to seeking
learning, to being a good citizen, a devotee of fine art

and so on. This is the only logical alternative to subordinating all aims to the accomplishment of one alone—
fanaticism. This is out of fashion at present, but who
can say how much of distraction and dissipation in life,
and how much of its hard and narrow rigidity is the
outcome of men's failure to realize that each situation
has its own unique end and that the whole personality
should be concerned with it? Surely, once more, what a
man needs is to live healthily, and this result so affects
all the activities of his life that it cannot be set up as
a separate and independent good.

Nevertheless the general notions of health, disease,
justice, artistic culture are of great importance: Not,
however, because this or that case may be brought ex-
haustively under a single head and its specific traits
shut out, but because generalized science provides a
man as physician and artist and citizen, with questions
to ask, investigations to make, and enables him to
understand the meaning of what he sees. Just in the
degree in which a physician is an artist in his work he
uses his science, no matter how extensive and accurate,
to furnish him with tools of inquiry into the individual
case, and with methods of forecasting a method of
dealing with it. Just in the degree in which, no matter
how great his learning, he subordinates the individual
case to some classification of diseases and some generic
rule of treatment, he sinks to the level of the routine

mechanic. His intelligence and his action become rigid, dogmatic, instead of free and flexible.

Moral goods and ends exist only when something has to be done. The fact that something has to be done proves that there are deficiencies, evils in the existent situation. This ill is just the specific ill that it is. It never is an exact duplicate of anything else. Consequently the good of the situation has to be discovered, projected and attained on the basis of the exact defect and trouble to be rectified. It cannot intelligently be injected into the situation from without. Yet it is the part of wisdom to compare different cases, to gather together the ills from which humanity suffers, and to generalize the corresponding goods into classes. Health, wealth, industry, temperance, amiability, courtesy, learning, esthetic capacity, initiative, courage, patience, enterprise, thoroughness and a multitude of other generalized ends are acknowledged as goods. But the *value* of this systematization is intellectual or analytic. Classifications *suggest* possible traits to be on the lookout for in studying a particular case; they suggest methods of action to be tried in removing the inferred causes of ill. They are tools of insight; their value is in promoting an individualized response in the individual situation.

Morals is not a catalogue of acts nor a set of rules to be applied like drugstore prescriptions or cook-book recipes.   The need in morals is for specific methods of inquiry and of contrivance: Methods of inquiry to locate difficulties and evils; methods of contrivance to form plans to be used as working hypotheses in dealing with them.   And the pragmatic import of the logic of individualized situations, each having its own irreplaceable good and principle, is to transfer the attention of theory from preoccupation with general conceptions to the problem of developing effective methods of inquiry.

Two ethical consequences of great moment should be remarked.   The belief in fixed values has bred a division of ends into intrinsic and instrumental, of those that are really worth while in themselves and those that are of importance only as means to intrinsic goods.   Indeed, it is often thought to be the very beginning of wisdom, of moral discrimination, to make this distinction.   Dialectically, the distinction is interesting and seems harmless.   But carried into practice it has an import that is tragic.   Historically, it has been the source and justification of a hard and fast difference between ideal goods on one side and material goods on the other. At present those who would be liberal conceive intrinsic goods as esthetic in nature rather than as exclusively religious or as intellectually contemplative.   But the effect is the same.   So-called intrinsic goods, whether religious or esthetic, are divorced from those interests

of daily life which because of their constancy and
urgency form the preoccupation of the great mass.
Aristotle used this distinction to declare that slaves and
the working class though they are necessary *for* the
state—the commonweal—are not constituents *of* it.
That which is regarded as *merely* instrumental must
approach drudgery; it cannot command either intellectual, artistic or moral attention and respect. Anything
becomes *unworthy* whenever it is thought of as intrinsically lacking worth. So men of " ideal " interests have
chosen for the most part the way of neglect and escape.
The urgency and pressure of " lower " ends have been
covered up by polite conventions. Or, they have been
relegated to a baser class of mortals in order that the
few might be free to attend to the goods that are really
or intrinsically worth while. This withdrawal, in the
name of higher ends, has left, for mankind at large and
especially for energetic " practical " people the lower
activities in complete command.

No one can possibly estimate how much of the obnoxious materialism and brutality of our economic life
is due to the fact that economic ends have been regarded as *merely* instrumental. When they are recognized to be as intrinsic and final in their place as any
others, then it will be seen that they are capable of
idealization, and that if life is to be worth while, they
must acquire ideal and intrinsic value. Esthetic, re-

ligious and other " ideal " ends are now thin and meagre
or else idle and luxurious because of the separation from
" instrumental " or economic ends.   Only in connection
with the latter can they be woven into the texture of
daily life and made substantial and pervasive.   The vanity and irresponsibility of values that are merely final
and not also in turn means to the enrichment of other
occupations of life ought to be obvious.   But now the
doctrine of " higher " ends gives aid, comfort and support to every socially isolated and socially irresponsible scholar, specialist, esthete and religionist.   It protects the vanity and irresponsibility of his calling from
observation by others and by himself.   The moral deficiency of the calling is transformed into a cause of
admiration and gratulation.

The other generic change lies in doing away once for
all with the traditional distinction between moral goods,
like the virtues, and natural goods like health, economic
security, art, science and the like.   The point of view
under discussion is not the only one which has deplored
this rigid distinction and endeavored to abolish it.   Some
schools have even gone so far as to regard moral excellencies, qualities of character as of value only because
they promote natural goods.   But the experimental
logic when carried into morals makes every quality
that is judged to be good according as it contributes
to amelioration of existing ills.   And in so doing, it

enforces the moral meaning of natural science. When all is said and done in criticism of present social deficiencies, one may well wonder whether the root difficulty does not lie in the separation of natural and moral science. When physics, chemistry, biology, medicine, contribute to the detection of concrete human woes and to the development of plans for remedying them and relieving the human estate, they become moral; they become part of the apparatus of moral inquiry or science. The latter then loses its peculiar flavor of the didactic and pedantic; its ultra-moralistic and hortatory tone. It loses its thinness and shrillness as well as its vagueness. It gains agencies that are efficacious. But the gain is not confined to the side of moral science. Natural science loses its divorce from humanity; it becomes itself humanistic in quality. It is something to be pursued not in a technical and specialized way for what is called truth for its own sake, but with the sense of its social bearing, its intellectual indispensableness. It is technical only in the sense that it provides the technique of social and moral engineering.

When the consciousness of science is fully impregnated with the consciousness of human value, the greatest dualism which now weighs humanity down, the split between the material, the mechanical, the scientific and the moral and ideal will be destroyed. Human forces that now waver because of this division will be

unified and reinforced. As long as ends are not thought
of as individualized according to specific needs and
opportunities, the mind will be content with abstractions, and the adequate stimulus to the moral or social
use of natural science and historical data will be
lacking. But when attention is concentrated upon the
diversified concretes, recourse to all intellectual materials
needed to clear up the special cases will be imperative.
At the same time that morals are made to focus in
intelligence, things intellectual are moralized. The
vexatious and wasteful conflict between naturalism and
humanism is terminated.

These general considerations may be amplified.
First: Inquiry, discovery take the same place in morals
that they have come to occupy in sciences of nature.
Validation, demonstration become experimental, a matter of consequences. Reason, always an honorific term
in ethics, becomes actualized in the methods by which
the needs and conditions, the obstacles and resources,
of situations are scrutinized in detail, and intelligent
plans of improvement are worked out. Remote and
abstract generalities promote jumping at conclusions,
" anticipations of nature." Bad consequences are then
deplored as due to natural perversity and untoward
fate. But shifting the issue to analysis of a specific
situation makes inquiry obligatory and alert observation of consequences imperative. No past decision ncr

old principle can ever be wholly relied upon to justify a course of action. No amount of pains taken in forming a purpose in a definite case is final; the consequences of its adoption must be carefully noted, and ƒ purpose held only as a working hypothesis until results confirm its rightness. Mistakes are no longer either mere unavoidable accidents to be mourned or moral sins to be expiated and forgiven. They are lessons in wrong methods of using intelligence and instructions as to a better course in the future. They are indications of the need of revision, development, readjustment. Ends grow, standards of judgment are improved. Man is under just as much obligation to develop his most advanced standards and ideals as to use conscientiously those which he already possesses. Moral life is protected from falling into formalism and rigid repetition. It is rendered flexible, vital, growing.

In the second place, every case where moral action is required becomes of equal moral importance and urgency with every other. If the need and deficiencies of a specific situation indicate improvement of health as the end and good, then for that situation health is the ultimate and supreme good. It is no means to something else. It is a final and intrinsic value. The same thing is true of improvement of economic status, of making a living, of attending to business and family demands—all of the things which under the sanction of fixed ends have been rendered of secondary and merely instrumental value, and so relatively base and unimportant. Anything that in a given situation is an end and good at all is of equal worth, rank and dignity with every other good of any other situation, and deserves the same intelligent attention.

We note thirdly the effect in destroying the roots of Phariseeism. We are so accustomed to thinking of this as deliberate hypocrisy that we overlook its intellectual premises. The conception which looks for the end of action within the circumstances of the actual situation will not have the same measure of judgment for all cases. When one factor of the situation is a person of trained mind and large resources, more will be expected than with a person of backward mind and uncultured experience. The absurdity of applying the same standard of moral judgment to savage peoples that is used with civilized will be apparent. No individual or group will be judged by whether they come up to or fall short of some fixed result, but by the direction in which they are moving. The bad man is the man who no matter how good he *has* been is beginning to deteriorate, to grow less good. The good man is the man who no matter how morally unworthy he *has* been is moving to become better. Such a conception makes one severe in judging himself and humane in judging others. It excludes that arrogance which always accompanies judgment based on degree of approximation to fixed ends.

In the fourth place, the process of growth, of improvement and progress, rather than the static outcome and result, becomes the significant thing. Not health as an end fixed once and for all, but the needed improvement in health—a continual process—is the end and good. The end is no longer a terminus or limit to be reached. It is the active process of transforming the existent situation. Not perfection as a final goal, but the ever-enduring process of perfecting, maturing, refining is the aim in living. Honesty, industry, temperance, justice, like health, wealth and learning, are not goods to be possessed as they would be if they expressed fixed ends to be attained. They are directions of change in the quality of experience. Growth itself is the only moral " end."

Although the bearing of this idea upon the problem of evil and the controversy between optimism and pessimism is too vast to be here discussed, it may be worth while to touch upon it superficially. The problem of evil ceases to be a theological and metaphysical one, and is perceived to be the practical problem of reducing, alleviating, as far as may be removing, the evils of life. Philosophy is no longer under obligation to find ingenious methods for proving that evils are only apparent, not real, or to elaborate schemes for explaining them away or, worse yet, for justifying them. It assumes another obligation:—That of contributing in however humble a way to methods that will assist us in discovering the causes of humanity's ills. Pessimism is a paralyzing doctrine. In declaring that the world is evil wholesale, it makes futile all efforts to discover the remediable causes of specific evils and thereby destroys at the root every attempt to make the world better and happier. Wholesale optimism, which has been the consequence of the attempt to explain evil away, is, however, equally an incubus.

After all, the optimism that says that the world is already the best possible of all worlds might be regarded as the most cynical of pessimisms. If this is the best possible, what would a world which was fundamentally bad be like? Meliorism is the belief that the specific conditions which exist at one moment, be they comparatively bad or comparatively good, in any event may be bettered. It encourages intelligence to study the positive means of good and the obstructions to their realization, and to put forth endeavor for the improvement of conditions. It arouses confidence and a reasonable hopefulness as optimism does not. For the latter in declaring that good is already realized in ultimate reality tends to make us gloss over the evils that concretely exist. It becomes too readily the creed of those who live at ease, in comfort, of those who have been successful in obtaining this world's rewards. Too readily optimism makes the men who hold it callous and blind to the sufferings of the less fortunate, or ready to find the cause of troubles of others in their personal vicious-ness. It thus co-operates with pessimism, in spite of the extreme nominal differences between the two, in benumbing sympathetic insight and intelligent effort in reform. It beckons men away from the world of relativity and change into the calm of the absolute and eternal.

The import of many of these changes in moral attitude focusses in the idea of happiness. Happiness has often been made the object of the moralists' contempt. Yet the most ascetic moralist has usually restored the idea of happiness under some other name, such as bliss. Goodness without happiness, valor and virtue without satisfaction, ends without conscious enjoyment—these things are as intolerable practically as they are self-contradictory in conception. Happiness is not, however, a bare possession; it is not a fixed attainment. Such a happiness is either the unworthy selfishness which moralists have so bitterly condemned, or it is, even if labelled bliss, an insipid tedium, a millennium of ease in relief from all struggle and labor. It could satisfy only the most delicate of molly-coddles. Happiness is found only in success; but success means succeeding, getting forward, moving in advance. It is an active process, not a passive outcome. Accordingly it includes the overcoming of obstacles, the elimination of sources of defect and ill. Esthetic sensitiveness and enjoyment are a large constituent in any worthy happiness. But the esthetic appreciation which is totally separated from renewal of spirit, from re-creation of mind and purification of emotion is a weak and sickly thing, destined to speedy death from starvation. That the renewal and re-creation come unconsciously not by set intention but makes them the more genuine.

Upon the whole, utilitarianism has marked the best in the transition from the classic theory of ends and goods to that which is now possible. It had definite merits. It insisted upon getting away from vague generalities, and down to the specific and concrete. It subordinated law to human achievement instead of subordinating humanity to external law. It taught that institutions are made for man and not man for institutions; it actively promoted all issues of reform. It made moral good natural, humane, in touch with the natural goods of life. It opposed unearthly and other worldly morality. Above all, it acclimatized in human imagination the idea of social welfare as a supreme test. But it was still profoundly affected in fundamental points by old ways of thinking. It never questioned the idea of a fixed, final and supreme end. It only questioned the current notions as to the nature of this end; and then inserted pleasure and the greatest possible aggregate of pleasures in the position of the fixed end.

Such a point of view treats concrete activities and specific interests not as worth while in themselves, or as constituents of happiness, but as mere external means to getting pleasures. The upholders of the old tradition could therefore easily accuse utilitarianism of making not only virtue but art, poetry, religion and the state into mere servile means of attaining sensuous enjoyments. Since pleasure was an outcome, a result valuable on its own account independently of the active processes that achieve it, happiness was a thing to be possessed and held onto. The acquisitive instincts of man were exaggerated at the expense of the creative. Production was of importance not because of the intrinsic worth of invention and reshaping the world, but because its external results feed pleasure. Like every theory that sets up fixed and final aims, in making the end passive and possessive, it made all active operations *mere* tools. Labor was an unavoidable evil to be minimized. Security in possession was the chief thing practically. Material comfort and ease were magnified in contrast with the pains and risk of experimental creation.

These deficiencies, under certain conceivable conditions, might have remained merely theoretical. But the disposition of the times and the interests of those who propagated the utilitarian ideas, endowed them with power for social harm. In spite of the power of the new ideas in attacking old social abuses, there were elements in the teaching which operated or protected to sanction new social abuses. The reforming zeal was shown in criticism of the evils inherited from the class system of feudalism, evils economic, legal and political. But the new economic order of capitalism that was superseding feudalism brought its own social evils with it, and some of these ills utilitarianism tended to cover up or defend. The emphasis upon acquisition and possession of enjoyments took on an untoward color in connection with the contemporary enormous desire for wealth and the enjoyments it makes possible.

If utilitarianism did not actively promote the new economic materialism, it had no means of combating it. Its general spirit of subordinating productive activity to the bare product was indirectly favorable to the cause of an unadorned commercialism. In spite of its interest in a thoroughly social aim, utilitarianism fostered a new class interest, that of the capitalistic property-owning interests, provided only property was obtained through free competition and not by governmental favor. The stress that Bentham put on security tended to consecrate the legal institution of private property provided only certain legal abuses in connection with its acquisition and transfer were abolished. *Beati possidentes*—provided possessions had been obtained in accord with the rules of the competitive game—without, that is, extraneous favors from government. Thus utilitarianism gave intellectual confirmation to all those tendencies which make " business " not a means of social service and an opportunity for personal growth in creative power but a way of accumulating the means of private enjoyments. Utilitarian ethics thus afford a remarkable example of the need of philosophic reconstruction which these lectures have been presenting. Up to a certain point, it reflected the meaning of modern thought and aspirations. But it was still tied down by fundamental ideas of that very order which it thought it had completely left behind: The idea of a fixed and single end lying beyond the diversity of human needs and acts rendered utilitarianism incapable of being an adequate representative of the modern spirit. It has to be reconstructed through emancipation from its inherited elements.

If a few words are added upon the topic of education, it is only for the sake of suggesting that the educative process is all one with the moral process, since the latter is a continuous passage of experience from worse to better. Education has been traditionally thought of as preparation: as learning, acquiring certain things because they will later be useful. The end is remote, and education is getting ready, is a preliminary to something more important to happen later on. Childhood is only a preparation for adult life, and adult life for another life. Always the future, not the present, has been the significant thing in education: Acquisition of knowledge and skill for future use and enjoyment; formation of habits required later in life in business, good citizenship and pursuit of science. Education is thought of also as something needed by some human beings merely because of their dependence upon others. We are born ignorant, unversed, unskilled, immature, and consequently in a state of social dependence. Instruction, training, moral discipline are processes by which the mature, the adult, gradually raise the helpless to the point where they can look out for themselves. The business of childhood is to grow into the independence of adulthood by means of the guidance of those who have already attained it. Thus the process of education as the main business of life ends when the young have arrived at emancipation from social dependence.

These two ideas, generally assumed but rarely explicitly reasoned out, contravene the conception that growing, or the continuous reconstruction of experience, is the only end. If at whatever period we choose to take a person, he is still in process of growth, then education is not, save as a by-product, a preparation for something coming later. Getting from the present the degree and kind of growth there is in it is education. This is a constant function, independent of age. The best thing that can be said about any special process of education, like that of the formal school period, is that it renders its subject capable of further education: more sensitive to conditions of growth and more able to take advantage of them. Acquisition of skill, possession of knowledge, attainment of culture are not ends: they are marks of growth and means to its continuing.

The contrast usually assumed between the period of education as one of social dependence and of maturity as one of social independence does harm. We repeat over and over that man is a social animal, and then confine the significance of this statement to the sphere in which sociality usually seems least evident, politics. The heart of the sociality of man is in education. The idea of education as preparation and of adulthood as a fixed limit of growth are two sides of the same obnoxious untruth. If the moral business of the adult as well as the young is a growing and developing experience, then the instruction that comes from social dependencies and interdependencies are as important for the adult as for the child. Moral independence for the adult means arrest of growth, isolation means induration. We exaggerate the intellectual dependence of childhood so that children are too much kept in leading strings, and then we exaggerate the independence of adult life from intimacy of contacts and communication with others. When the identity of the moral process with the processes of specific growth is realized, the more conscious and formal education of childhood will be seen to be the most economical and efficient means of social advance and reorganization, and it will also be evident that the test of all the institutions of adult life is their effect in furthering continued education. Government, business, art, religion, all social institutions have a meaning, a purpose. That purpose is to set free and to develop the capacities of human individuals without respect to race, sex, class or economic status. And this is all one with saying that the test of their value is the extent to which they educate every individual into the full stature of his possibility. Democracy has many meanings, but if it has a moral meaning, it is found in resolving that the supreme test of all political institutions and industrial arrangements shall be the contribution they make to the all-around growth of every member of society.

CHAPTER VIII

RECONSTRUCTION AS AFFECTING SOCIAL PHILOSOPHY

How can philosophic change seriously affect social philosophy? As far as fundamentals are concerned, every view and combination appears to have been formulated already. Society is composed of individuals: this obvious and basic fact no philosophy, whatever its pretensions to novelty, can question or alter. Hence these three alternatives: Society must exist for the sake of individuals; or individuals must have their ends and ways of living set for them by society; or else society and individuals are correlative, organic, to one another, society requiring the service and subordination of individuals and at the same time existing to serve them. Beyond these three views, none seems to be logically conceivable. Moreover, while each of the three types includes many subspecies and variations within itself, yet the changes seem to have been so thoroughly rung that at most only minor variations are now possible.

Especially would it seem true that the " organic " conception meets all the objections to the extreme individualistic and extreme socialistic theories, avoiding the errors alike of Plato and Bentham. Just because society is composed of individuals, it would seem that individuals and the associative relations that hold them together must be of coequal importance. Without strong and competent individuals, the bonds and ties that form society have nothing to lay hold on. Apart from associations with one another, individuals are isolated from one another and fade and wither; or are opposed to one another and their conflicts injure individual development. Law, state, church, family, friendship, industrial association, these and other institutions and arrangements are necessary in order that individuals may grow and find their specific capacities and functions. Without their aid and support human life is, as Hobbes said, brutish, solitary, nasty.

We plunge into the heart of the matter, by asserting that these various theories suffer from a common defect. They are all committed to the logic of general notions under which specific situations are to be brought. What we want light upon is this or that group of individuals, this or that concrete human being, this or that special institution or social arrangement. For such a logic of inquiry, the traditionally accepted logic substitutes discussion of the meaning of concepts and their dialectical relationship to one another. The discussion goes on in terms of *the* state, *the* individual; the nature of institutions as such, society in general.

We need guidance in dealing with particular perplexities in domestic life, and are met by dissertations on the Family or by assertions of the sacredness of individual Personality. We want to know about the worth of the institution of private property as it operates under given conditions of definite time and place. We meet with the reply of Proudhon that property generally is theft, or with that of Hegel that the realization of will is the end of all institutions, and that private ownership as the expression of mastery of personality over physical nature is a necessary element in such realization. Both answers may have a certain suggestiveness in connection with specific situations. But the conceptions are not proffered for what they may be worth in connection with special historic phenomena. They are general answers supposed to have a universal meaning that covers and dominates all particulars. Hence they do not assist inquiry. They close it. They are not instrumentalities to be employed and tested in clarifying concrete social difficulties. They are ready-made principles to be imposed upon particulars in order to determine their nature. They tell us about *the* state when we want to know about *some* state. But the implication is that what is said about *the* state applies to any state that we happen to wish to know about.

In transferring the issue from concrete situations to definitions and conceptual deductions, the effect, espe-

cially of the organic theory, is to supply the apparatus
for intellectual justification of the established order.
Those most interested in practical social progress and
the emancipation of groups from oppression have turned
a cold shoulder to the organic theory.   The effect, if not
the intention, of German idealism as applied in social
philosophy was to provide a bulwark for the maintenance of the political *status quo* against the tide of
radical ideas coming from revolutionary France.   Although Hegel asserted in explicit form that the end of
states and institutions is to further the realization of
the freedom of all, his effect was to consecrate the Prussian State and to enshrine bureaucratic absolutism.
Was this apologetic tendency accidental, or did it
spring from something in the logic of the notions that
were employed?

Surely the latter.   If we talk about *the* state and *the*
individual, rather than about this or that political organization and this or that group of needy and suffering
human beings, the tendency is to throw the glamor and
prestige, the meaning and value attached to the general
notion, over the concrete situation and thereby to cover
up the defects of the latter and disguise the need of serious reforms.   The meanings which are found in the general notions are injected into the particulars that come
under them.   Quite properly so if we once grant the
logic of rigid universals under which the concrete cases

have to be subsumed in order to be understood and explained.

Again, the tendency of the organic point of view is to minimize the significance of specific conflicts. Since the individual and the state or social institution are but two sides of the same reality, since they are already reconciled in principle and conception, the conflict in any particular case can be but apparent. Since in theory the individual and the state are reciprocally necessary and helpful to one another, why pay much attention to the fact that in *this* state a whole group of individuals are suffering from oppressive conditions? In " reality " their interests cannot be in conflict with those of the state to which they belong; the opposition is only superficial and casual. Capital and labor cannot " really " conflict because each is an organic necessity to the other, and both to the organized community as a whole. There cannot " really " be any sex-problem because men and women are indispensable both to one another and to the state. In his day, Aristotle could easily employ the logic of general concepts superior to individuals to show that the institution of slavery was in the interests both of the state and of the slave class. Even if the intention is not to justify the existing order the effect is to divert attention from special situations. Rationalistic logic formerly made men careless in observation of the concrete in physical philosophy. It now operates to depress and retard observation in specific social phenomena. The social philosopher, dwelling in the region of his concepts, " solves " problems by showing the relationship of ideas, instead of helping men solve problems in the concrete by supplying them hypotheses to be used and tested in projects of reform.

Meanwhile, of course, the concrete troubles and evils remain. They are not magically waived out of existence because in theory society is organic. The region of concrete difficulties, where the assistance of intelligent method for tentative plans for experimentation is urgently needed, is precisely where intelligence fails to operate. In this region of the specific and concrete, men are thrown back upon the crudest empiricism, upon short-sighted opportunism and the matching of brute forces. In theory, the particulars are all neatly disposed of; they come under their appropriate heading and category; they are labelled and go into an orderly pigeon-hole in a systematic filing cabinet, labelled political science or sociology. But in empirical fact they remain as perplexing, confused and unorganized as they were before. So they are dealt with not by even an endeavor at scientific method but by blind rule of thumb, citation of precedents, considerations of immediate advantage, smoothing things over, use of coercive force and the clash of personal ambitions. The world still survives; it has therefore got on somehow:—so much cannot be denied. The method of trial and error and competition of selfishnesses has somehow wrought out many improvements. But social theory nevertheless exists as an idle luxury rather than as a guiding method of inquiry and planning. In the question of methods concerned with reconstruction of special situations rather than in any refinements in the general concepts of institution, individuality, state, freedom, law, order, progress, etc., lies the true impact of philosophical reconstruction.

Consider the conception of the individual self. The individualistic school of England and France in the eighteenth and nineteenth centuries was empirical in intent. It based its individualism, philosophically speaking, upon the belief that individuals are alone real, that classes and organizations are secondary and derived. They are artificial, while individuals are natural. In what way then can individualism be said to come under the animadversions that have been passed? To say the defect was that this school overlooked those connections with other persons which are a part of the constitution of every individual is true as far as it goes; but unfortunately it rarely goes beyond the point of just that wholesale justification of institutions which has been criticized.

The real difficulty is that the individual is regarded as something *given*, something already there. Consequently, he can only be something to be catered to, something whose pleasures are to be magnified and possessions multiplied. When the individual is taken as something given already, anything that can be done to him or for him it can only be by way of external impressions and belongings: sensations of pleasure and pain, comforts, securities. Now it is true that social arrangements, laws, institutions are made for man, rather than that man is made for them; that they are means and agencies of human welfare and progress. But they are not means for obtaining something for individuals, not even happiness. They are means of *creating* individuals. Only in the physical sense of physical bodies that to the senses are separate is individuality an original datum. Individuality in a social and moral sense is something to be wrought out. It means initiative, inventiveness, varied resourcefulness, assumption of responsibility in choice of belief and conduct. These are not gifts, but achievements. As achievements, they are not absolute but relative to the use that is to be made of them. And this use varies with the environment.

The import of this conception comes out in considering the fortunes of the idea of self-interest. All members of the empirical school emphasized this idea. It was the sole motive of mankind. Virtue was to be attained by making benevolent action profitable to the

individual; social arrangements were to be reformed so
that egoism and altruistic consideration of others would
be identified. Moralists of the opposite school were not
backward in pointing out the evils of any theory that
reduced both morals and political science to means of
calculating self-interest. Consequently they threw the
whole idea of interest overboard as obnoxious to morals.
The effect of this reaction was to strengthen the cause
of authority and political obscurantism. When the
play of interest is eliminated, what remains? What
concrete moving forces can be found? Those who identified the self with something ready-made and its interest with acquisition of pleasure and profit took the
most effective means possible to reinstate the logic of
abstract conceptions of law, justice, sovereignty, freedom, etc.—all of those vague general ideas that for all
their seeming rigidity can be manipulated by any clever
politician to cover up his designs and to make the worse
seem the better cause. Interests are specific and dynamic; they are the natural terms of any concrete social
thinking. But they are damned beyond recovery when
they are identified with the things of a petty selfishness.
They can be employed as vital terms only when the
self is seen to be in process, and interest to be a
name for whatever is concerned in furthering its movement.

The same logic applies to the old dispute of whether

reform should start with the individual or with institutions. When the self is regarded as something complete within itself, then it is readily argued that only internal moralistic changes are of importance in general reform. Institutional changes are said to be merely external. They may add conveniences and comforts to life, but they cannot effect moral improvements. The result is to throw the burden for social improvement upon free-will in its most impossible form. Moreover, social and economic passivity are encouraged. Individuals are led to concentrate in moral introspection upon their own vices and virtues, and to neglect the character of the environment. Morals withdraw from active concern with detailed economic and political conditions. Let us perfect ourselves within, and in due season changes in society will come of themselves is the teaching. And while saints are engaged in introspection, burly sinners run the world. But when self-hood is perceived to be an active process it is also seen that social modifications are the only means of the creation of changed personalities. Institutions are viewed in their educative effect:—with reference to the types of individuals they foster. The interest in individual moral improvement and the social interest in objective reform of economic and political conditions are identified. And inquiry into the meaning of social arrangements gets definite point and direction. We are led to ask what the specific stimulating, foster-

ing and nurturing power of each specific social arrangement may be. The old-time separation between politics
and morals is abolished at its root.

Consequently we cannot be satisfied with the general
statement that society and the state is organic to the
individual. The question is one of specific causations.
Just what response does *this* social arrangement, political or economic, evoke, and what effect does it
have upon the disposition of those who engage in it?
Does it release capacity? If so, how widely? Among
a few, with a corresponding depression in others, or in
an extensive and equitable way? Is the capacity which
is set free also directed in some coherent way, so that
it becomes a power, or its manifestation spasmodic and
capricious? Since responses are of an indefinite diversity of kind, these inquiries have to be detailed and
specific. Are men's senses rendered more delicately sensitive and appreciative, or are they blunted and dulled
by this and that form of social organization? Are their
minds trained so that the hands are more deft and cun-
ning? Is curiosity awakened or blunted? What is its
quality: is it merely esthetic, dwelling on the forms and
surfaces of things or is it also an intellectual searching into their meaning? Such questions as these (as
well as the more obvious ones about the qualities conventionally labelled moral), become the starting-points
of inquiries about every institution of the community

when it is recognized that individuality is not originally given but is created under the influences of associated life. Like utilitarianism, the theory subjects every form of organization to continual scrutiny and criticism. But instead of leading us to ask what it does in the way of causing pains and pleasures to individuals already in existence, it inquires what is done to release specific capacities and co-ordinate them into working powers. What sort of individuals are created?

The waste of mental energy due to conducting discussion of social affairs in terms of conceptual generalities is astonishing. How far would the biologist and the physician progress if when the subject of respiration is under consideration, discussion confined itself to bandying back and forth the concepts of organ and organism: —If for example one school thought respiration could be known and understood by insisting upon the fact that it occurs in an individual body and therefore is an " individual " phenomenon, while an opposite school insisted that it is simply one function in organic interaction with others and can be known or understood therefore only by reference to other functions taken in an equally general or wholesale way? Each proposition is equally true and equally futile. What is needed is specific inquiries into a multitude of specific structures and interactions. Not only does the solemn reiteration of categories of individual and organic or social whole not further these definite and detailed inquiries, but it checks them. It detains thought within pompous and sonorous generalities wherein controversy is as inevitable as it is incapable of solution. It is true enough that if cells were not in vital interaction with one another, they could neither conflict nor co-operate. But the fact of the existence of an " organic " social group, instead of answering any questions merely marks the fact that questions exist: Just what conflicts and what co-operations occur, and what are their specific causes and consequences? But because of the persistence within social philosophy of the order of ideas that has been expelled from natural philosophy, even sociologists take conflict or co-operation as general categories upon which to base their science, and condescend to empirical facts only for illustrations. As a rule, their chief " problem " is a purely dialectical one, covered up by a thick quilt of empirical anthropological and historical citations: How do individuals unite to form society? How are individuals socially controlled? And the problem is justly called dialectical because it springs from antecedent conceptions of " individual " and " social."

Just as " individual " is not one thing, but is a blanket term for the immense variety of specific reactions, habits, dispositions and powers of human nature that are evoked, and confirmed under the influences of associated life, so with the term " social." Society is one word, but infinitely many things. It covers all the ways in which by associating together men share their experiences, and build up common interests and aims; street gangs, schools for burglary, clans, social cliques, trades unions, joint stock corporations, villages and international alliances. The new method takes effect in substituting inquiry into these specific, changing and relative facts (relative to problems and purposes, not metaphysically relative) for solemn manipulation of general notions.

Strangely enough, the current conception of the state is a case in point. For one direct influence of the classic order of fixed species arranged in hierarchical order is the attempt of German political philosophy in the nineteenth century to enumerate a definite number of institutions, each having its own essential and immutable meaning; to arrange them in an order of " evolution " which corresponds with the dignity and rank of the respective meanings. The National State was placed at the top as the consummation and culmination, and also the basis of all other institutions.

Hegel is a striking example of this industry, but he is far from the only one. Many who have bitterly quarrelled with him, have only differed as to the details of the " evolution " or as to the particular meaning to be attributed as essential *Begriff* to some one of the enumerated institutions. The quarrel has been bitter only because the underlying premises were the same. Particularly have many schools of thought, varying even more widely in respect to method and conclusion, agreed upon the final consummating position of the state. They may not go as far as Hegel in making the sole meaning of history to be the evolution of National Territorial States, each of which embodies more than the prior form of the essential meaning or conception of *the* State and consequently displaces it, until we arrive at that triumph of historical evolution, the Prussian State. But they do not question the unique and supreme position of the State in the social hierarchy. Indeed that conception has hardened into unquestionable dogma under the title of sovereignty.

There can be no doubt of the tremendously important rôle played by the modern territorial national state. The formation of these states has been the centre of modern political history. France, Great Britain, Spain were the first peoples to attain nationalistic organization, but in the nineteenth century their example was followed by Japan, Germany and Italy, to say nothing of a large number of smaller states, Greece, Servia, Bulgaria, etc. As everybody knows, one of the most important phases of the recent world war was the struggle to complete the nationalistic movement, resulting in the erection of Bohemia, Poland, etc., into independent states, and the accession of Armenia, Palestine, etc., to the rank of candidates.

The struggle for the supremacy of the State over other forms of organization was directed against the power of minor districts, provinces, principalities, against the dispersion of power among feudal lords as well as, in some countries, against the pretensions of an ecclesiastic potentate. The " State " represents the conspicuous culmination of the great movement of social integration and consolidation taking place in the last few centuries, tremendously accelerated by the concentrating and combining forces of steam ad electricity. Naturally, inevitably, the students of political science have been preoccupied with this great historic phenomenon, and their intellectual activities have been directed to its systematic formulation. Because the contemporary progressive movement was to establish the unified state against the inertia of minor social units and against the ambitions of rivals for power, political theory developed the dogma of the sovereignty of the national state, internally and externally.

As the work of integration and consolidation reaches its climax, the question arises, however, whether the national state, once it is firmly established and no longer struggling against strong foes, is not just an instrumentality for promoting and protecting other and more voluntary forms of association, rather than a supreme

end in itself. Two actual phenomena may be pointed to
in support of an affirmative answer. Along with the
development of the larger, more inclusive and more unified organization of the state has gone the emancipation
of individuals from restrictions and servitudes previously imposed by custom and class status. But the individuals freed from external and coercive bonds have not
remained isolated. Social molecules have at once recom-
bined in new associations and organizations. Compul-
sory associations have been replaced by voluntary ones;
rigid organizations by those more amenable to human
choice and purposes—more directly changeable at will.
What upon one side looks like a movement toward individualism, turns out to be really a movement toward
multiplying all kinds and varieties of associations:
Political parties, industrial corporations, scientific and
artistic organizations, trade unions, churches, schools,
clubs and societies without number, for the cultivation of
every conceivable interest that men have in common. As
they develop in number and importance, the state tends
to become more and more a regulator and adjuster
among them; defining the limits of their actions, preventing and settling conflicts.

Its " supremacy " approximates that of the con-
ductor of an orchestra, who makes no music himself but
who harmonizes the activities of those who in producing
it are doing the thing intrinsically worth while. The

state remains highly important—but its importance consists more and more in its power to foster and co-ordinate the activities of voluntary groupings. Only nominally is it in any modern community the end for the sake of which all the other societies and organizations exist. Groupings for promoting the diversity of goods that men share have become the real social units. They occupy the place which traditional theory has claimed either for mere isolated individuals or for the supreme and single political organization. Pluralism is well ordained in present political practice and demands a modification of hierarchical and monistic theory. Every combination of human forces that adds its own con-tribution of value to life has for that reason its own unique and ultimate worth. It cannot be degraded into a means to glorify the State. One reason for the increased demoralization of war is that it forces the State into an abnormally supreme position.

The other concrete fact is the opposition between the claim of independent sovereignty in behalf of the terri-torial national state and the growth of international and what have well been called trans-national interests. The weal and woe of any modern state is bound up with that of others. Weakness, disorder, false principles on the part of any state are not confined within its boun-daries. They spread and infect other states. The same is true of economic, artistic and scientific advances.

Moreover the voluntary associations just spoken of do not coincide with political boundaries. Associations of mathematicians, chemists, astronomers; business corporations, labor organizations, churches are trans-national because the interests they represent are worldwide. In such ways as these, internationalism is not an aspiration but a fact, not a sentimental ideal but a force. Yet these interests are cut across and thrown out of gear by the traditional doctrine of exclusive national sovereignty. It is the vogue of this doctrine, or dogma, that presents the strongest barrier to the effective formation of an international mind which alone agrees with the moving forces of present-day labor, commerce, science, art and religion.

Society, as was said, is many associations not a single organization. Society means association; coming together in joint intercourse and action for the better realization of any form of experience which is augmented and confirmed by being shared. Hence there are as many associations as there are goods which are enhanced by being mutually communicated and participated in. And these are literally indefinite in number. Indeed, capacity to endure publicity and communication is the test by which it is decided whether a pretended good is genuine or spurious. Moralists have always insisted upon the fact that good is universal, objective, not just private, particular. But too often, like Plato, they have been content with a metaphysical universality or, like Kant, with a logical universality. Communication, sharing, joint participation are the only actual ways of universalizing the moral law and end. We insisted at the last hour upon the unique character of every intrinsic good. But the counterpart of this proposition is that the situation in which a good is consciously realized is not one of transient sensations or private appetites but one of sharing and communication—public, social. Even the hermit communes with gods or spirits; even misery loves company; and the most extreme selfishness includes a band of followers or some partner to share in the attained good. Universalization means socialization, the extension of the area and range of those who share in a good.

The increasing acknowledgment that goods exist and endure only through being communicated and that association is the means of conjoint sharing lies back of the modern sense of humanity and democracy. It is the saving salt in altruism and philanthropy, which without this factor degenerate into moral condescension and moral interference, taking the form of trying to regulate the affairs of others under the guise of doing them good or of conferring upon them some right as if it were a gift of charity. It follows that organization is never an end in itself. It is a means of promoting *asso-*

ciation, of multiplying effective points of contact between persons, directing their intercourse into the modes of greatest fruitfulness.

The tendency to treat organization as an end in itself is responsible for all the exaggerated theories in which individuals are subordinated to some institution to which is given the noble name of society. Society is the *process* of associating in such ways that experiences, ideas, emotions, values are transmitted and made common. To this active process, both the individual and the institutionally organized may truly be said to be subordinate. The individual is subordinate because except in and through communication of experience from and to others, he remains dumb, merely sentient, a brute animal. Only in association with fellows does he become a conscious centre of experience. Organization, which is what traditional theory has generally meant by the term Society or State, is also subordinate because it becomes static, rigid, institutionalized whenever it is not employed to facilitate and enrich the contacts of human beings with one another.

The long-time controversy between rights and duties, law and freedom is another version of the strife between the Individual and Society as fixed concepts. Freedom for an individual means growth, ready change when modification is required.

It signifies an active process, that of release of

capacity from whatever hems it in. But since society can develop only as new resources are put at its disposal, it is absurd to suppose that freedom has positive significance for individuality but negative meaning for social interests. Society is strong, forceful, stable against accident only when all its members can function to the limit of their capacity. Such functioning cannot be achieved without allowing a leeway of experimentation beyond the limits of established and sanctioned custom. A certain amount of overt confusion and irregularity is likely to accompany the granting of the margin of liberty without which capacity cannot find itself. But socially as well as scientifically the great thing is not to avoid mistakes but to have them take place under conditions such that they can be utilized to increase intelligence in the future.

If British liberal social philosophy tended, true to the spirit of its atomistic empiricism, to make freedom and the exercise of rights ends in themselves, the remedy is not to be found in recourse to a philosophy of fixed obligations and authoritative law such as characterized German political thinking. The latter, as events have demonstrated, is dangerous because of its implicit menace to the free self-determination of other social groups. But it is also weak internally when put to the final test. In its hostility to the free experimentation and power of choice of the individual in determining social affairs, it limits the capacity of many or most individuals to share effectively in social operations, and thereby deprives society of the full contribution of all its members. The best guarantee of collective efficiency and power is liberation and use of the diversity of individual capacities in initiative, planning, foresight, vigor and endurance. Personality must be educated, and personality cannot be educated by confining its operations to technical and specialized things, or to the less important relationships of life. Full education comes only when there is a responsible share on the part of each person, in proportion to capacity, in shaping the aims and policies of the social groups to which he belongs. This fact fixes the significance of democracy. It cannot be conceived as a sectarian or racial thing nor as a consecration of some form of government which has already attained constitutional sanction. It is but a name for the fact that human nature is developed only when its elements take part in directing things which are common, things for the sake of which men and women form groups—families, industrial companies, governments, churches, scientific associations and so on. The principle holds as much of one form of association, say in industry and commerce, as it does in government. The identification of democracy with political democracy which is responsible for most of its failures is, however, based upon the traditional ideas which make the individual and the state ready-made entities in themselves.

As the new ideas find adequate expression in social life, they will be absorbed into a moral background, and will the ideas and beliefs themselves be deepened and be unconsciously transmitted and sustained. They will color the imagination and temper the desires and affections. They will not form a set of ideas to be expounded, reasoned out and argumentatively supported, but will be a spontaneous way of envisaging life. Then they will take on religious value. The religious spirit will be revivified because it will be in harmony with men's unquestioned scientific beliefs and their ordinary day-by-day social activities. It will not be obliged to lead a timid, half-concealed and half-apologetic life because tied to scientific ideas and social creeds that are continuously eaten into and broken down. But especially will the ideas and beliefs themselves be deepened and intensified because spontaneously fed by emotion and translated into imaginative vision and fine art, while they are now maintained by more or less conscious effort, by deliberate reflection, by taking thought. They are technical and abstract just because they are not as yet carried as matter of course by imagination and feelings.

We began by pointing out that European philosophy arose when intellectual methods and scientific results moved away from social traditions which had consolidated and embodied the fruits of spontaneous desire and fancy. It was pointed out that philosophy had ever since had the problem of adjusting the dry, thin and meagre scientific standpoint with the obstinately persisting body of warm and abounding imaginative beliefs. Conceptions of possibility, progress, free movement and infinitely diversified opportunity have been suggested by modern science. But until they have displaced from *imagination* the heritage of the immutable and the once-for-all ordered and systematized, the ideas of mechanism and matter will lie like a dead weight upon the emotions, paralyzing religion and distorting art. When the liberation of capacity no longer seems a menace to organization and established institutions, something that cannot be avoided practically and yet something that is a threat to conservation of the most precious values of the past, when the liberating of human capacity operates as a socially creative force, art will not be a luxury, a stranger to the daily occupations of making a living. Making a living economically speaking, will be at one with making a life that is worth living. And when the emotional force, the mystic force one might say, of communication, of the miracle of shared life and shared experience is spontaneously felt, the hardness and crudeness of contemporary life will be bathed in the light that never was on land or sea.

Poetry, art, religion are precious things. They cannot be maintained by lingering in the past and futilely wishing to restore what the movement of events in science, industry and politics has destroyed. They are an out-flowering of thought and desires that unconsciously converge into a disposition of imagination as a result of thousands and thousands of daily episodes and contact. They cannot be willed into existence or coerced into being. The wind of the spirit bloweth where it listeth and the kingdom of God in such things does not come with observation. But while it is impossible to retain and recover by deliberate volition old sources of religion and art that have been discredited, it is possible to expedite the development of the vital sources of a religion and art that are yet to be. Not indeed by action directly aimed at their production, but by substituting faith in the active tendencies of the day for dread and dislike of them, and by the courage of intelligence to follow whither social and scientific changes direct us. We are weak today in ideal matters because intelligence is divorced from aspiration. The bare force of circumstance compels us onwards in the daily detail of our beliefs and acts, but our deeper thoughts and desires turn backwards. When philosophy shall have co-operated with the course of events and made clear and coherent the meaning of the daily detail, science and emotion will interpenetrate, practice and imagination will embrace. Poetry and religious feeling will be the unforced flowers of life. To further this articulation and revelation of the meanings of the current course of events is the task and problem of philosophy in days of transition.

INDEX

Absolute reality, 23, 27

Absolutism, 97, 190; Kant and, 99

Abstract definition, 20

Abstractions, 149-150, 174

Absurdities, 10

Achievements, 194

Action, kind of, 80

Adult life, 185, 186

America, 41

Amoeba, 91

Animals, dramatisation in primitive life of man, 4

Antiquity, 33

Apprehension, 142

Aquinas, 55, 106

Argumentation, 31, 132

Aristotle, 13, 17, 19, 55; Bacon's charge against, 30-31, 36; distinction in ends, 171; experience, 79, 80; forms, 105; on change, 107; on philosophy as contemplation, 109, 110; on slavery, 191; theory of the state, 44; ultimate reality, 106

Art, 34, 103, 211, 212

Artisan, 15; knowledge, 110

Associations, 205; voluntary, 203

Astronomers, 65, 113

Astronomy, 75

Athenians, 13, 19

Augustine, St., 111

Authority, 48, 139, 195; final, 161; seat of, 160. *See also* Final good

Bacon, Francis, 28, 81, 97; criticism of the learning of his day, 29-30; experience, 97-98; "knowledge is power," 29; summary of ideas, 29

Being, perfect, 111

Being and non-being, 107

Beliefs and facts, 12

Bentham, 166, 182, 188

Bergson, 71

Berkeley, 50

Biology, 75, 84

Bliss, 111, 112

Bosanquet, 134

Bradley, 107

Bruno, 66

Business, 41, 43, 183

Butler, Bishop, 21

Capital, 43

Capital and labour, 191

Capitalism, 41, 182

Castes, material, 59

Casuistry, 166

Causation, 63

Causes, 59, 60

Certainty, 21, 22

Change, ancient idea of, 57; existing view, 113; law of the universe, 61; Plato and Aristotle on, 107; progress and, 116

Chemistry, 75

Child life, 91-92, 184

Christian mediaeval philosophy, 17, 19

Christian theology, 111

Church, 47; universal, 45

Classes, 75, 152, 155; in the ancient conception of the world, 59